Australian Sports J

CW00508360

This insightful volume explores the major challenges facing sports journalism in Australia today, discussing how, in an environment dominated by sports organisations and increasing commercial factors, the role of the sports journalist is being severely compromised.

By combining quantitative and qualitative responses from 120 sports journalists with previous research and placing these in the theoretical lenses of field and gatekeeping theories, this book provides a comprehensive overview of the field of Australian sports journalism. Topics discussed include ethical questions in reporting on sports, the role of women in sports journalism, and the increased commercialisation of the field, as well as journalists' perceptions on sports organisations and the changing access for media. The book also offers suggestions for the future of the industry, and two contemporary conceptual models are developed.

Offering important insight into the workings of contemporary sports journalism in Australia, this book is a useful resource for academics and students around the world in the fields of journalism, media, sports and communication.

Peter English is an academic and journalist who has spent the past two decades working in sports journalism. He is Senior Lecturer at the University of the Sunshine Coast, Australia. His main research area is sports journalism, and he continues to write for domestic and international publications.

Australian Sports Journalism

Power, Control and Threats

Peter English

Routledge
Taylor & Francis Group

LONDON AND NEW YORK

First published 2021
by Routledge
2 Park Square, Milton Park, Abingdon, Oxon OX14 4RN

and by Routledge
52 Vanderbilt Avenue, New York, NY 10017

Routledge is an imprint of the Taylor & Francis Group, an informa business

British Library Cataloguing-in-Publication Data
A catalogue record for this book is available from the British Library

Library of Congress Cataloging-in-Publication Data
Names: English, Peter, (Professor of journalism) author.
Title: Australian sports journalism : power, control, and threats / Peter English.
Description: London ; New York : Routledge, 2021. | Series: Routledge studies in journalism | Includes bibliographical references and index.
Identifiers: LCCN 2020031802 | ISBN 9780367857813 (hardback) | ISBN 9781003015048 (ebook)
Subjects: LCSH: Sports journalism—Australia.
Classification: LCC PN4784.S6 E54 2021 | DDC 070.4/497960994—dc23
LC record available at https://lccn.loc.gov/2020031802

ISBN: 978-0-367-85781-3 (hbk)
ISBN: 978-1-003-01504-8 (ebk)

Typeset in Times New Roman
by Apex CoVantage, LLC

Contents

Tables and figures

Tables

Figures

Acknowledgements

As a former full-time sports journalist, I have experienced some of the ethical dilemmas and situations outlined in this book. It was not written from a position of purity but produced to record what has been happening in the industry, through the views of its journalists, in the hope improvements can be made to ensure sports journalism's long-term health. As Beijing Foreign Studies University Professor Wei Wei argues, it is the job of sports media scholars to scrutinise sports journalism. This book has been written with this aim in mind.

There are many people who have helped with this project (USC ethics approval number A181139). The work of Ed Reddin and Richard Bond as research assistants was vital in conducting the survey. I also want to acknowledge the domestic and international peer reviewers, both from the academy and industry, for their invaluable comments on versions of each chapter. My colleagues at USC have been particularly supportive and always listen politely to my sports stories. Folker Hanusch has provided excellent tips from start to finish. Finally, to the two home-schoolers who assisted with editing, comments and mostly timely interruptions, this is for you. Maybe you will flick through it one day.

1 Australian sports journalism in a global context

Sports journalism around the world has undergone significant recent change and the industry continues to experience a wide range of threats that challenge its traditional existence. In an environment increasingly dominated by sports organisations and pervasive commercial factors, the role of sports journalism and the practices of its journalists have been severely compromised. This has forced considerable shifts for journalists, as well as audiences and the broader sporting community, in the way they receive and interpret information. In many Western nations, sports journalism is a shadow of what it has been historically, indicating the contemporary environment is in crisis following transformations in online delivery and economic conditions over the past decade, and the increased power of sports and commercial organisations. For journalists and, more broadly, audiences, key threats include control of information, access to key figures, commercial ties impacting on decisions, and the diminishing role of critically examining teams, athletes and issues. This results in more sanitised coverage of sport, greater public-relations driven content in the sports pages and on broadcasts, and a reduced understanding of wider sporting issues. It also raises questions about ethical decisions taken by sports journalists in this new environment. Crucially, the situation has created a loss of journalistic capital, which is critical in an industry increasingly dominated by big business.

Australian sports journalism is the focus of this book that analyses threats being faced both in this country and other media systems. Outlining some of these influences will expose the dangers that the dominance of the sports industry has created for media organisations. While these examples are concentrated on the Australian context, they will provide useful insight for other nations and newsrooms experiencing similar issues (see Billings 2019; English 2016a; McEnnis 2018; Mirer 2019). Key areas involve the development of sports organisations and their media management and in-house platforms, and the rise of commercial factors in which business decisions can overrule journalistic ones. Combined with changing newsroom structures in Australia, including fewer staff and higher workloads (see ACCC 2019; Doran 2020; Hutchins & Boyle 2017; O'Donnell et al. 2016; Sherwood & O'Donnell 2018), these factors create an environment where there is potential for the erosion of traditional ethics. As a result, the conditions in the field are threatening both the current status and the future of sports journalism. It is therefore vital that they are outlined and analysed, including suggestions for the future of sports reporting.

The platform for this analysis is data from a survey of 120 sports journalists in Australian mainstream, metropolitan newsrooms. These interviews occurred before the spread of Covid-19, and at the time of writing the long-term impact of the virus on sport, sports organisations and media was still unknown. Combining the primary quantitative and qualitative responses with previous research and commentary, as well as discussion through the theoretical lenses of field and gatekeeping theories, provides a comprehensive overview of the field of Australian sports journalism. The data will be utilised in chapters outlining the commercialisation of sports journalism and sports organisations' dominance of sports journalism in the country. Based on these results, suggestions for the future of the industry in Australia will be outlined, particularly in relation to retaining independence and relevance in an environment currently dominated by major sporting businesses. Finally, two conceptual models of sports journalism in Australia will be discussed. By outlining the traits, characteristics and areas of concern, these results can be utilised to highlight experiences that may either be happening in other sports newsrooms around the globe, or able to inform them, by providing insight into the workings of contemporary sports journalism.

Australia's place in the sporting world

Australia is a small country in terms of international power, but in sporting terms its athletes and teams have often exceeded expectations in the global arena. Along with a strong fan following, this has contributed to a reputation for being a sporting nation (Lawe-Davies & Le Brocque 2006; Ward 2015; Zion et al. 2011). Australia has top 10 finishes on the medal tally at the Olympics between 1992 and 2016, despite having a population of less than 26 million (ABS 2020), and recent World Championship status in mainstream sports, such as cricket, rugby union and cycling, and more niche sports, including netball, surfing and snooker. The nation is also consumed, particularly in winter, by Australian rules football and rugby league, highlighting its wide interest in specific sports. At each step, tackle and pass, the media report on the successes and failures of club, state and national teams, and individuals within them. Sports coverage can dominate news pages and broadcasts. Shoemaker and Cohen (2006) found sports stories were the most popular type of news in Australia, with 20.7% of content devoted to sport. In this ten-country study, it placed Australia alongside the United States and South Africa in having sport as the primary topic of news. This approach to reporting on sport is not new in Australia, with Mayer (1964) finding more sport than politics in newspapers. However, the sports and news areas have evolved considerably since both of these studies, particularly with the continued rise of digital media, as well as structural changes within the sports and sports journalism fields, including the financial power of sports organisations.

When examining a nation such as Australia, it is important to recognise the relationships between its media system and those of other nations. Geographically, Australia is located in the Global South (Wasserman 2014) and has a Commonwealth history, sharing a colonial background with nations such as India and Canada, and therefore strong ties to the United Kingdom. While Australia has close proximity and developing links with many Asian nations, it has also been described as a Western journalism culture, along with having attributes of the North Atlantic, or liberal model, of media systems, placing it alongside the United States, the United Kingdom and Canada (Hallin & Mancini 2004; Hanitzsch et al. 2010). In this context, the findings of this analysis of Australian sports journalism offer insight for other nations and media systems with similar characteristics. Australia's close links with the reporting of sport in other Western, Commonwealth, Global South and Asian nations mean the results and discussions are relevant to other markets either experiencing similar problems, or seeing them on the horizon. Since the Global Financial Crisis there have been massive contractions in Western newsrooms, with up to 3000 Australian journalists losing their jobs since the first effects of the GFC (ACCC Digital Platforms Inquiry 2018). This has created reduced budgets, rounds of redundancies, fewer staff and changing publications (Doran 2020; O'Donnell et al. 2016; Sherwood & O'Donnell 2018). Unsurprisingly, the situation has impacted heavily on sports journalism, with greater workloads for continuing staff, reduced ability to travel to games, more reporting off the television instead of attending events, and broader content deals to fill sports pages and bulletins. The evolving work practices have also led to changes to traditional aspects such as ethics (see English 2016c). All of these negative events were occurring at a time when the sports industry and many of the organisations the sports journalists were reporting on were expanding their financial footprints and gaining greater economic capital, (notwithstanding the stoppages created by the Covid-19 pandemic in 2020). This altered the power structures and affected the place of sports journalism within the sports and journalistic fields, both in Australia and elsewhere. What has been occurring in Australia is relevant from both domestic and international perspectives.

What is sports journalism?

One of the overarching issues occurring in broader journalism around the world is whether the media delivers public interest or entertainment journalism. This is particularly the case in sport and the issue has been magnified with the continued dominance of online media, where clicks and analytics often determine the agenda. Sport has traditionally been more focused on entertainment and less on critical elements (Boyle 2006; Boyle & Haynes 2009; Rowe 2007; Zion et al. 2011), given that it predominantly deals with entertainment itself, such as results of games, or the performances or predictions of those involved in these contests. Similarly, the view of sports journalists is often described as trivial, or low status, with the reporters operating in the "toy department" of the newsroom, and an area often focusing on celebrity and promotion (Boyle 2017; Boyle et al. 2012; Mason 2000; McEnnis 2018; Rowe 2007; Zion et al. 2011). But it is unfair to dismiss the work of sports journalists as unimportant or trivial. Successful sports reporting combines public interest with entertainment. The work of sports reporters has always been valuable in informing, educating and entertaining, and while it does not result in the over-throwing of tyrannical governments, or the exposing of state secrets, at its best it plays a crucial role in highlighting truth in public-interest organisations, providing critical analysis and doing it in a way that is also entertaining. Sections of sports journalism, of course, have a history of beautiful writing, particularly in the United Kingdom and the United States (see Boyle 2017; English 2016b).

The Australian Competition and Consumer Commission, in its Digital Platforms Inquiry Final Report (ACCC 2019), outlines how the definition of public service journalism can include reporting on corruption or criminal behaviour in sport, in contrast to the reporting of results. Sports journalism at times holds a public service role, but investigations and critical enquiry have often been ignored or avoided (see Boyle & Haynes 2009; Henningham 1995; Steen 2011; Rowe 2004, 2007). In the contemporary environment, with its economic restrictions, there is even less scope for this type of reporting. While investigative journalism provides new, public interest material, it is incredibly expensive due to reporters having to spend extended periods on one story or issue. In the United Kingdom, *The Guardian* publishes work from investigative sports reporter David Conn, but these posts are rare and often on top of other regular reporting. David Walsh, from *The Sunday Times* in the United Kingdom, has undertaken major investigative work on drugs in cycling, with his reports exposing the doping of Lance Armstrong. In-depth sports investigations are often likely to appear on "news" programs, such as the BBC's *Panorama*, or Germany's *ARD*, particularly on topics such as drugs in sport. This occurred on *Panorama* in 2019 with the revelations of coach Alberto Salazar and the Nike Oregon Project. Critical work is a foundation of sports journalism, but one that is often overlooked in a news environment constantly churning through "breaking news" content. There is less of an investigative sport focus in Australia, but there has been sustained reporting in match-fixing in cricket, drug use in the Australian Football League, and doping in horse racing. It is important to note that much of this reporting involved sports journalists operating as part of their regular "round" rather than sustained work by a standalone investigative reporter.

Sports journalists are often criticised as cheerleaders for their teams as opposed to being traditional, independent and objective journalists in the watchdog mode (see English 2018). Some of the descriptions of sports journalists are fans, boosters, biased, and sychophants, who are producing scrapbook material (see Anderson 2001; Billings et al. 2011; Boyle et al. 2012; Garrison & Salwen 1989; Hardin 2005; Marchetti 2005; McEnnis 2016; Rowe 2004). This type of approach can also involve promoting the home team, being uncritical of players, exaggerating the mistakes or "attacking" the "away" side (see English 2017), and feeling like they are part of the team. In previous eras, this was literally the case, with sports journalists travelling or staying with the players and officials (Anderson 2001; Blake 2012). This has led to this sub-section of the industry being viewed as less professional and, as a result, less ethical, most notably in relation to honesty, fairness and independence. In traditional journalism, objectivity, independence and critical watchdog roles are considered crucial (Boyle et al. 2012; Hardin 2005; Hardin et al. 2009; Mindich 1998; Rowe 2004; Schudson 2001; Tuchman 1972). As Boyle et al. (2012) note, there can be confusion over the roles of sports journalists, and whether they are operating as reporters or fans, which leads to ethical questions over balanced reporting (see Hardin 2005). Aspects involving both cheerleading and investigations are examined in the survey results of the Australian sports journalists and provide an important guide to other areas of the world.

Many journalists consider it demeaning to be described as a cheerleader, with *Wisden* editor Lawrence Booth (2013, p. 5) writing it is a great insult to be accused of being a "fan with a laptop". The late *The Guardian* sports writer Frank Keating (2001) described Australian journalists as being a "band of one-eyed fans with laptops and microphones" during the Ashes series that year, causing anger within the visiting media ranks. However, Hardin (2005) stated almost 40% of sports editors in United States newspapers felt the sports pages should cheer the home sides. English (2017) examined content and sports journalists' responses from Australia and India, finding a focus on home team coverage. However, Indian journalists were more likely to describe themselves as fans than Australian reporters.

It is important to note the aim for sports journalists – and journalists over-all – to be literally neutral is unreachable, and total objectivity is no lon-ger expected by audiences (see Billings in Ramon 2016; Hallin & Mancini 2004; Weedon & Wilson 2017). Ramon (2016) argues there is a subjective element in sports reporting that cannot be avoided, which is supported by Steen (2015, p. 10), who states the job involves impartiality but also the need "to be one-eyed". However, the scale of the commercial influence in contemporary media has grown to challenge the independence and detach-ment of journalists and newsrooms from sports and external organisations. Boyle and Haynes (2009) suggest sports journalism focuses on aspects of reporting, enquiring and explaining sports issues and events, and thinking of audiences when holding sports to account. In this environment, it is valu-able to outline the roles of sports journalists in Australia, as well as the threats to sports journalism in the nation.

Ethics and sports journalism

A key ethical aspect of media in many parts of the world is independence, which links with media freedom. It is a characteristic detailed in codes of ethics and codes of conduct in, for example, the United States, the United Kingdom and India (National Union of Journalists 2019; Press Council of India 2018; Society of Professional Journalists 2019). In Australia, jour-nalists following the MEAA (2020) Code of Ethics commit themselves to reporting independently, honestly, fairly, respecting the public's right to information, and respecting truth. Independence involves not being tied to governments and officials in general journalism, but also applies to sports journalism and the relationship of newsrooms and journalists to sports organ-isations and commercial entities, which can result in compromises to the purity of information being delivered. This is becoming more complex when sports organisations or in-house sites have their own publishing plat-forms, which do not have to be balanced or fair, and therefore appeal to sup-porters who only want to read positive or carefully framed stories that suit their clubs, teams or athletes. Attempts to cosy up to the business and com-mercial elements in sport can be made in an attempt to gain more access. This has occurred in other nations (English 2016b) and contravenes ethical guidelines.

In Australia, journalists do not allow "advertising or other commercial considerations to undermine accuracy, fairness or independence"; in India advertisements "must be clearly distinguishable from news content" (Press Council of India 2018); and in the United Kingdom there is no endorsing of advertisements or commercial products (National Union of Journalists 2019). Journalists in the United States are told to "deny favored treatment to advertisers, donors or any other special interests, and resist internal and external pressure to influence coverage" (Society of Professional Journalists 2019). This is becoming more difficult in an environment in which commercial factors and sports organisations have developed greater economic capital and dominate news organisations in the sports journalism field. It is important to recognise that sports journalism has been important to the business of media, particularly in terms of newspapers gaining readers, circulation and revenue (see Boyle 2017; Boyle & Haynes 2009; Hargreaves 1986; Hutchins & Boyle 2017; Horky & Stelzner 2013; Nicholson et al. 2015). Apart from government-funded organisations, such as the Australian Broadcasting Corporation (ABC) or the BBC in the United Kingdom, external commercial factors are crucial considerations. In the contemporary environment these factors are having a greater impact on sports journalism. As a result, the approaches towards independence of sports journalists in Australia can provide a useful guide to other nations, including how they are acting in ethical terms, and be utilised to suggest ways to ensure the future of reporting operates in an appropriate manner.

Audience demands are part of the commercial space and can influence which team is focused on predominantly in coverage, and therefore skews towards the local side (see, for example, Billings et al. 2011; English 2017). The reporting is often favourable. Now, it is important to note that teams deserve praise when they perform well, but also justify criticism when performing poorly. While this is an issue for sports journalists directly, it is also magnified by the hordes of former players who crowd broadcast commentary boxes and often operate as promotional mouthpieces. This may be to do with their close allegiance to their former teams, the contractual need to be positive in their delivery, or due to conflicts of interests in their other roles. For example, the former England cricket captain Michael Vaughan was criticised by batsman Jonathan Trott for his comments that suggested he was supporting players in the same sports management firm representing him (BBC 2016).

The issue is also seen in the conflict over athletes and officials sponsored by commercial organisations, which result in changed or heavily sanitised public positions. Another example from England is the former marathon world record holder Paula Ratcliffe. Ratcliffe was an anti-doping campaigner during her career but was not overly critical when United States-based coach Alberto Salazar was banned for four years due to doping violations. Ratcliffe had been commentating during the BBC's coverage of the 2019 World Championships, but was sponsored by Nike – whose Nike Oregon Project training facility was run by Salazar – and married to the coach of Mo Farah, a four-time Olympic gold medallist previously coached by Salazar. In a controversial interview on the BBC, Ratcliffe played down the suspension of Salazar and her commercial and personal links to the coach were not mentioned (Holt 2019; Ronay 2019). As Holt (2019) wrote, Ratcliffe's response was "heavy with the weight of vested interests and corporate loyalties". Similar issues were raised through comments by fellow BBC pundit and former athlete Steve Cram.

Another example occurred during the 2019 cricket World Cup, when the West Indian commentator Michael Holding was reprimanded by the International Cricket Council's broadcast rights holder, Sunset + Vine, for describing the umpiring as "atrocious" (Harman 2019). He was told the role of host broadcasters was "not to judge or highlight mistakes". These types of "mistakes" are a crucial part of the narrative of the game, providing moments for critical reporting on a range of on-field issues. In his reported reply, Holding, a former fast bowler from the 1970s and '80s, said commentators were "being more and more compromised by controlling organisations to the point of censorship" (Harman 2019). At the 2020 Australian Open, Tennis Australia stopped the live broadcast of a protest by John McEnroe and Martina Navratilova when they spoke out against the divisive same-sex views of former champion Margaret Court, who has an arena named after her (*news.com.au* 2020). Australian commentator Geoff Lemon (in Harman 2019) noted how similar constraints were applied in India, where the Board for Control of Cricket in India (BCCI) outlines what can and cannot be said in commentary. The rise of the Indian Premier League, and the power of the BCCI has created multiple conflicts of interest and sanitising of content. Harsha Bhogle, the prominent broadcaster, was at one time a commentator for the league and an advisor for the Mumbai Indians team. He was sacked from the IPL in 2016, with reports suggesting his work was not focusing enough on Indian players (Sawai 2017).

In Australian cricket, in particular, there are many former players-turned-broadcasters who wear multiple caps, an issue discussed in Chapter 2. While these examples do not always involve athletes-turned-journalists – past players have moved into reporting, particularly in England, and focus on more balanced accounts – they often get merged within the media sport space. The work of all in sports media therefore impacts on the sports journalism field. It is clear that reporting and interpreting independently is crucial to avoid – or at least ease – the control currently being exerted by sports organisations and commercial factors. It is also vital in presenting information in an ethical way. As mentioned, entertainment is a crucial element to sports reporting, but is complemented by publications providing new and different information. These examples highlight both commercial and sporting conflict through the presence of former athletes, particularly in broadcasts, but similar aspects are infiltrating other areas of the Australian sports journalism landscape.

Sports journalism in Australia – a short history

In comparison with many nations in the Global North, Australia has a relatively short history of journalism. After being colonised by Great Britain in 1788, Australian newspapers did not begin formally until 1803, with *The Sydney Gazette and New South Wales Advertiser*. Sports coverage, including extensive reporting of cricket, was printed from the 1830s (Cashman 1995). The horse-racing-focused *Bell's Life* began in 1845 and *The Referee*, the first newspaper in the country specifically for sport, started in 1886 and "reflected the craze for sports results and information" (Cashman 1995; Stoddart 1986, p. 89). In an early example of sport's links with commercial elements, Miller et al. (2007) state sports media developed in Australia and the United Kingdom through notices about upcoming sports events, as well as reports on matches and hospitality – and betting (see Walker 2006). Coverage of sport in print was regularly included in the late 1800s and the start of the 1900s (Mayer 1964; Stoddart 1986), highlighting the growing importance of this subfield to publishing and audiences.

In the second half of the 19th century, sports coverage in Australia – and around the world – was boosted by the introduction of the telegraph, which allowed news agencies to distribute results across the globe (Goldlust 1987). This was occurring at a time when sports publications were increasing, and issues around identity and professionalism were developing that continue to this day. Sports journalist William Corbett started on *The Referee* and in 1913 was *The Sun*'s sports editor (Stoddart 1986). At the time, Corbett (in Stoddart 1986, p. 89) noted the importance of sport as "a serious public concern", recognising that "good sports writing would sell newspapers". He also stated that while sport was good for the business of newspapers, highlighting the importance of internal commercial and financial elements, it was also important as sport itself. The fight for the legitimacy has been a historical battle that continues in contemporary newsrooms (see Coward 2015), where sports journalists are often dismissed as playing games (for examples see Boyle et al. 2012; Rowe 2007).

The introduction of radio in Australia in the 1920s created disruption for newspaper reporters, who were now often passing on news that had already been broadcast (Boyle & Haynes 2009; Stoddart 1986). This set a pattern for changes to print journalism, which later suffered through the introduction of television in the 1950s and the internet in the 1990s. The ABC's first ball-by-ball radio broadcast occurred during the Bodyline series in 1932–1933, before synthetic broadcasts based on telegraph cables were used for the following year's Ashes tour (Andrewes 2000). One impact the development of radio had on print was changing the reports from producing information to articles describing "personality status and entertainment" (Stoddart 1986,

p. 95). Later this included bylines with the writer's actual name, rather than a pseudonym or job title. These were used in Australia from the 1930s and considered a way to develop personalities in newspapers (Stoddart 1986).

Further changes to the news environment arrived with television, which was introduced for the 1956 Olympics in Melbourne. When colour television arrived in 1975 it quickly became the most popular medium, and created huge changes in the way sport was viewed and reported. The introduction of World Series Cricket, which was developed by the media mogul Kerry Packer in the 1970s, transformed the way sport was presented, as well as highlighting the commercial benefits of broadcast rights. These developments provided a space for sports-specific television news and feature shows, such as *Wide World of Sports*, *Sportsworld* and *Sports Tonight*. The introduction of pay television in 1995, through Optus and Foxtel, created another player in the broadcast market, which again turned the focus on commercialisation of sport through rights and subscription fees for audiences. Radio has continued to be a popular place for sport, including on weekends on ABC Grandstand. SEN in Victoria gained a licence to broadcast sport 24 hours a day in 2003, and more recently Macquarie Sports Radio started in 2017, although these platforms have regular challenges and audience changes as part of the digital disruption running through the rest of the media industry (see Jackson 2017; *The Age* 2003).

The most recent major change has occurred through the rise of the internet, with online and digital threatening all traditional media. The web's arrival in the 1990s changed sports departments by providing more technological features, unlimited space for content, increased workloads and – at first – more staff (Boyle & Haynes 2009; English 2010; Steen 2008). Newspaper publications were slow to adapt online, with *The Age* starting a website in 1995 but not, as Nguyen (2008) states, experimenting with serious online sports coverage until the 2004 Olympics (see also Van Heekeran 2010). Non-print publications slowly joined the online space, including Ninemsn in 1997 (Van Heekeran 2010), which continued the move towards niche publications in sport, such as baggygreen.com.au, which was hosted by a cricket publisher, *Cricinfo*, and for a time was also the official site of Cricket Australia. The commercial-sports organisation deal ran into trouble when stories unfavourable to the sporting body were published first on its "own" website. This occurred when Darren Lehmann, who would go on to coach Australia, shouted racist remarks in the dressing room after being dismissed in a match against Sri Lanka, and when batsman Justin Langer was described in commentary as a "brown nose gnome" (*The Sydney Morning Herald* 2003; *The Age* 2004). The speed of work also changed, with exclusive stories lasting minutes – at least until social media arrived, when the scoop could be limited to the few seconds it took for a retweet or repost.

These challenges have been experienced around the world, but increased following the Global Financial Crisis, with falling revenues resulting in declining budgets and staff.

These substantial technological and structural changes in the Australian media system resulted in greater workloads, alterations in content and the focus on different platforms, and an increase in commercial factors (see Boyle & Haynes 2009; English 2014b; Hutchins & Boyle 2017). Hutchins and Rowe (2012, p. 125) described sports journalism as a "leaking craft" following the convergence of new media and expanding digital media and corporate players. These developments, along with increased competition across media, including social media, dedicated sports websites and the products of sports organisations themselves, have created increasing pressures and forces in the sports journalism field. The changes – in Australia and other parts of the world – have caused greater transformations in the industry than over the previous 50 years. The damage was first applied to print, and has since become more prevalent in some areas of television. As an example, due to financial constraints, newspaper sports journalism is no longer a job where reporters are dispatched to sporting fields to send short newspaper reports. That role is now often replaced by sports journalists watching matches and press conferences on television, or relying on news agency or syndicated reports.

Standalone websites, which sometimes focus on single sports, have gained popularity and are often supported by international companies, such as ESPN. More concerning for sports journalism is that sports organisations themselves have entered the market as publishers, with their own staff operating as commercial or club "journalists" for in-house websites and social media channels. They often gain guaranteed – or at least easier – access to key subjects because both the "reporter" and source are staff members and on the same team. Athlete-only sites have also emerged, such as *Players-Voice* and *AthletesVoice*, which has been similar to *The Players' Tribune* in the United States, offering single-sourced, unscrutinised and copy-approved content. As a result of the wide-ranging developments in sport and general media, mainstream sports journalism has shrunk in Australia. In this context, it is vital to examine the threats within the Australian sports journalism field, which can provide insight to both domestic and international markets undergoing similar transformations.

Examining contemporary Australian journalism

To help understand sports journalism in this changing environment, a survey was undertaken with 120 sports journalists working in Australian capital-city-based media organisations across print, online, radio, television and news agencies. The quantitative and qualitative responses form the basis of the results and discussion in the remainder of the book, and help provide practical examples and responses to the threats and challenges to the industry. The survey builds on the work of Henningham (1995) and Nicholson et al. (2011), who surveyed Australian sports journalists to develop a profile of the profession. At a theoretical level, the data will be examined in relation to gatekeeping theory and field theory, providing an examination of the choices, influences, forces and threats impacting sports journalists in Australia. Field theory (Bourdieu 1984, 1998) is an important tool, with its ability to locate forces within the field, including those actors who are dominant and dominated. This is particularly relevant in relation to commercial factors, with journalism as a whole suffering financially over the past decade, and the potential for organisations and journalists to make concessions to the market, pursing economic capital instead of journalistic capital. Contests over capital are a feature of the journalistic field, with economic capital dominant (Benson & Neveu 2005; Bourdieu 1998). Journalistic capital can combine different forms of capital, such as cultural, symbolic and social, as well as highlighting power, position, prestige and social legitimacy (Hovden 2008; Meyen & Riesmeyer 2012; Vos et al. 2019). Gatekeeping theory is also valuable in this analysis as it can highlight where and how decisions are being made in relation to commercial factors, ethics and the impact of sports organisations. These forces and influences can occur at individual, routines, organisational or broader societal levels (see Shoemaker & Vos 2009). Individual journalists have personal and professional backgrounds and beliefs that impact their decisions, while routines include professional guidelines as well as roles and patterns of behaviour (Shoemaker & Vos 2009; White 1950). At the organisational level, the company employs journalists as gatekeepers, and sets the rules and direction over journalistic or economic aims, while broader societal levels involve external influences such as government, commercial elements, media systems and sources (Breed 1955; English 2014b; Shoemaker & Vos 2009).

The approach to the survey method in this book is the same used by English (2019). Following an extensive population sampling process (see Hanusch 2015; Hanusch & Bruns 2017), it was estimated there were approximately 600 sports journalists in Australia employed in these newsrooms. The sample was developed through database searching through *Margaret Gee's Australian Media Guide* (2018), newspaper and online bylines, and reporting appearances on broadcast and social media. While there have been changes to sub-editing and production in newsrooms since the decline in media revenues, there are roles that are not publicly visible. As English (2019) described, measures were taken to address this to ensure an accurate estimate of the population and a representative sample in the categories of publication medium, gender and geography. However, with an absence of official data on the number of sports journalists working in Australia, the population remains an estimate and is a limitation of the study.

Following the call of Nicholson et al. (2011) to undertake further research into what defines a sports journalist, the following definition has been developed: a sports journalist is a professional who undertakes a combination of elements, including writing, interviewing, producing, editing, commenting or presenting about sports contests, athletes, officials or issues (see also English 2019). In addition to this definition, journalists had to have been working in a media organisation that had its own sports section or program to be included in the survey. Journalists at each level of the organisations were part of the sample, including freelancers – as long as they were aligned professionally with a newsroom (see English 2019). Sports journalists must have been working for a media organisation that was independent of sports organisations or government agencies. Media included the areas of print, television, radio, online, magazines, and news agencies. To ensure a greater range of responses, no more than five sports journalists from any one newsroom were included in the final sample. However, due to the ownership concentration of media, more than five sports journalists were included from the same parent company (e.g. News Corp Australia, Fairfax Media/Nine, the ABC). Once the population was established, entries of sports journalists were stratified into the categories of medium, gender and geography, to ensure a representative sample from these elements. Random lists were then generated and surveys were undertaken by the author and two research assistants. Phone surveys were completed between September 2018 and May 2019, with the 120 respondents ensuring a sample of 20% of the estimated population. The interviews occurred before the emergence of Covid-19 and, as a result, this issue was not addressed in their comments. The response rate was 35.8%, with a total of 342 sports journalists approached. Respondents were asked questions across 80 categories, with the quantitative and qualitative data utilised to understand the threats being faced by Australian sports journalists.

The field of play

Sports journalism is often viewed as simple but it operates in an increasingly complex field. Previously, sports journalism occurred in print, television and radio, but since the explosion of the internet the landscape has changed dramatically, splintering audiences and giving fans a myriad of ways to find their news, views or promotional material. In this space, sports journalism remains important but has been compromised. It has to be noted that sport has been seen traditionally as what Boyle (2017, p. 493) describes as a "promoter of sport and its culture" rather than where the "powerful" are called to account. This places it in conflict at times with the traditional, independent roles of detached journalism (see Mindich 1998; Schudson 2001; Tuchman 1972), and can involve "compromise or journalistic complicity" with players and officials in the sports industry (see also Boyle & Haynes 2009; Horky & Nieland 2013; Schultz-Jorgensen 2005; Rowe 2007). However, Boyle (2006, p. 125) states that promotion "is simply not what sports journalism is about", and it is "winning and success on the field of play that remains the most important driver in shaping journalistic opinion and comment". This remains a key comment for sports journalists and future sports journalists to consider in their work. When necessary, sports journalists praise and criticise, but they remain independent, publishing information that is freely available, but can also be hidden. They comment and scrutinise, develop sources and, crucially, are detached from the commercial forces that are becoming so pervasive in modern media. The findings in this book can assist budding sports journalists in providing an understanding of the industry and avenues into newsrooms of the future. While the focus is on Australia, the results and discussion are also relevant to sports journalists and newsrooms around the world who experience these factors in similar ways.

2 The field of Australian sports journalism

Sports journalism has been a key subfield of the journalistic field in Australia for more than a century. The field operates within the broader Australian media system, but has become an important space for its contribution towards society, news-gathering and publishing. However, the area has experienced considerable change due to working conditions, financial instability and the growth of the broader sports industry and the sports field. These pressures and changing forces have had a major influence on a space that was historically dominant in determining the types of information readers, viewers and listeners received. An increasing number of online publications, the fragmenting of audiences, and rises in the economic capital of sports organisations have altered these structures, providing new challenges for sports journalism and its journalists. Through this analysis of Australian sports journalists in this chapter, the roles and threats of sports journalists in contemporary newsrooms are explored alongside the overall media environment. This is valuable in gaining an understanding of what those working in the industry consider both important and threatening in contemporary sports journalism.

The media system in Australia

Sports journalism in Australia operates in a media system that has a decentralised market, which is geographically dispersed across capital cities around the nation. At the same time, it is highly concentrated in terms of ownership and operating structures across major mediums and publications, which creates issues for diversity of information, and the potential for corporate conflicts of interest. In legacy print-based organisations, there are three main companies: News Corp Australia, Fairfax Media (now called Nine) and Seven News Media. These businesses control the mainstream capital-city print and online titles across Australia, but also operate increasingly across media. As well as owning established newspapers and websites, News Corp Australia, the company started by Rupert Murdoch, is a majority shareholder in pay television operators Foxtel and Fox Sports. This combination creates major conflict and political-economy issues in general media, sports journalism and broadcast rights. Fox Sports controls a range of pay-tv channels and bids for a variety of sporting rights, while also hosting a multi-sports website. Fox Sports' parent company, News Corp Australia, owns the Sky News channel, a 24-hour operation, which appears on Foxtel as well as free-to-air television through WIN in regional Australia. The company was a shareholder in the news agency Australian Associated Press until its sale in 2020, when it started its own NCA Newswire. Further, it is an investor in the Brisbane Broncos rugby league team, an arrangement which raises huge ethical problems with the coverage provided in particular by News Corp Australia's Queensland newspaper and online publications, *The Courier-Mail* and *The Sunday Mail*. The Nine corporation controls a major free-to-air television company, radio stations, print and online products following the merger with Fairfax Media in 2018. Seven West Media, which is owned by Kerry Stokes, operates the national television station Seven while also managing magazines, through its Pacific Magazines arm, and Western Australian-based newspaper publications. The other main free-to-air television stations are Ten, the ABC and SBS, with the latter two funded by the federal government.

The ABC employs a large number of sports journalists for its news, commentary and feature programs across television, radio and online. Online is both a large area of the Australian market, with the importance of a web presence for all traditional publications, and a smaller niche area through single-sport websites. These can be from international operations with an Australian presence, such as *ESPNcricinfo* or *ESPNscrum*, or standalone sites such as *The Roar*, which was bought by the company behind *Athletes-Voice* in 2019. Specialist magazines form part of the field, either as titles of larger companies, such as *Inside Sport*, or independent publications, which can focus on non-mainstream sports like mountain biking, surfing or lawn bowls. A small but essential area of the Australian sports journalism system is news agencies. Australian Associated Press is the largest employer of journalists in this sector, providing wide-ranging but straight coverage for regional, metropolitan and national publications. International agencies Reuters, Associated Press and Agence France-Presse rely on an extremely small number of staff and a pool of freelancers to cover stories predominantly for overseas markets. Sport is a major topic across these platforms, with dedicated news, feature and results-focused content, and specialist material that appears across multi-media news outlets.

The value of Australian sports journalism

Sports journalism in Australia is important for many reasons that cover journalistic, business and societal reasons. Australia has been described as a sports-obsessed nation (Zion et al. 2011) and the games and contests are part of its national identity (Coward 2015). There is a desire for audiences to read, watch and listen to match reports, news and analysis. Sports content is a fixture of media publications – only the *Australian Financial Review* does not have a dedicated sports section of the major Australian media outlets – and reflects both the interest and importance of this area of the field. Telling a fan or a supporter that you are a sports journalist often results in descriptions of jealousy or envy, as well as feedback on the latest mistake in your reporting. But the broader view of sports journalism and its journalists is often devalued, both in industry and academia (Boyle 2006; Henningham 1995; Nicholson et al. 2011; Schultz 2005). When sports journalist Mike Coward (2015) received an Australian Sports Council lifetime achievement award after more than half a century of reporting, he said it had long "irked" him that sports writing in Australia had "been devalued", especially in comparison with its higher standing in the United Kingdom and the United States. He noted some of the best Australian writing had been in sport and hoped in the future sports writing would be regarded more highly.

Sports writing regularly gains large amounts of space in traditional media, which has often been more than reporting on topics such as politics (Boyle 2006; Lawe-Davies & Le Brocque 2006; Mayer 1964; Shoemaker & Cohen 2006). Newspapers and websites have sports sections while television and radio news bulletins have dedicated sports segments. Sports newsrooms have contained the highest number of specialised journalists in the country (Henningham 1998; Nicholson et al. 2011). While the readership and ratings have declined in legacy media in Australia (Fisher et al. 2019), there has been an increase in the number of published articles on sport since 2001 (ACCC 2019). This shift highlights the desire of audiences for coverage. Sports journalism is also valuable to the business of newspapers, with it being used to attract readers and revenue (Boyle & Haynes 2009; Hargreaves 1986; Horky & Stelzner 2013; Nicholson et al. 2015). This approach applies particularly to the commercial operations, which rely on advertisers and audiences, whether as viewers or subscribers. The broader sports industry has expanded rapidly over the past couple of decades, with rights deals now being measured in the billions of dollars. Sports journalism should play an important role in scrutinising these huge amounts of money criss-crossing through the hands of athletes, administrators and managers. In this context, it is clear that sports journalism is important to the journalistic field, and its practices and publications deserve analysis, as well as protecting.

Sports journalism is now conducted in an environment that has become considerably more difficult for journalists, with increased workloads, declining levels of staff, reduction in access to players, and greater infiltration of commercial aspects. This situation is reflective of other changes in media over the past two decades, including practitioners being in "a life constantly on the edge of chaos" (Deuze 2007, p. 43). In days gone by, players could be spoken to in the dressing room with ease. Coward (2015) said he once interviewed Viv Richards while the West Indian cricket great was in bed, and Dennis Lillee while he was having a bath. Access to players in current times is much more sanitised, with reporters often unlikely to interact with athletes outside of stage-managed press conferences. This can create division between the two groups, with little chance for understanding what the other side is trying to achieve. Alternatively, this distance should provide greater detachment from the subjects, and more independent reporting, although due to the increasing power of sports organisations this is often not the case. With the restrictions in place in the contemporary landscape for sports journalists, the best a reporter may be able to do is watch a live feed of a press conference on television, or copy quotes from a press release or agency report, or rely on second-hand information to produce a story. In many cases, the changing roles have resulted in sports journalism in Australia being less rigorous, more public-relations driven, less independent and more homogenous. It is a situation in which both sports journalists and the audience lose.

The business of sport

Sport's rise from pastime to staple of television broadcasts to multi-platform mega coverage has created a dramatic shift in the power structures of the sports journalism and sports fields. Changes are not only linked to money, but also to the power and influence generated by organisations – both sporting administrative bodies and those aligned with the game, such as sponsors. Through their commercial strength, organisations can determine who gains access to athletes or matches, which media outlets are given preferred treatment over story or interview opportunities, how they are catered for, and whether a particular media outlet is offered advertisements. At the time of writing, the lasting impacts of Covid-19 and the disruptions to sport and the relationships between sports organisations and media were still being played out. However, there were significant reductions in staff and budgets in sports organisations of large and small sports, including AFL, cricket, rugby union, rugby league and netball (see, for example, Gleeson & Niall 2020; Harris 2020; Keoghan et al. 2020; Lalor 2020a).

In the past, sports newsrooms had more flexibility in what requests they accommodated, including running stories on a particular event, or attending a sponsor's function, or not covering a specific story. With declining financial resources and audience figures (Fisher et al. 2019), the changes to industry, including greater fragmentation in media products in the shift to online and social media, have left the legacy publications with reduced power to influence sports organisations and their decisions. In many cases, news companies take anything they are offered in an effort to gain an advantage over rivals, or stay in the publishing race. This shift highlights how commercial factors are the dominant capital in the sports field (see Benson & Neveu 2005; Bourdieu 1998), with money, access and advantage likely to dominate many journalistic elements.

Previously, sports organisations relied on media coverage to boost attendance and revenue, but the size of rights deals in sport has driven riches into the major competitions in Australia. The NRL agreed a $1.8 billion TV deal from 2018 to 2022 (ABC 2015), the AFL negotiated a $2.5 billion broadcast arrangement for 2017–2022 (Fox Sports 2015) and Cricket Australia earned $1.2 billion over six years from 2018 (Letts 2018). The cricket agreement resulted in significant changes to the televising of the game, which had been Nine's domain since World Series Cricket in the 1970s. Under the new conditions, Seven and Foxtel shared coverage. These developments highlight some of the issues and conflicts of interest that have the potential to affect sports journalists, athletes and sports organisations at a macro level. Sport is unusual in media in that its companies pay to host sporting content, rather than covering it for free like other news departments. With the large amounts of money spent on rights comes organisational directives and constraints that lead to dilemmas over what content or stories sports journalists should include – or ignore. In Australia, with the structure of major news companies spanning multiple media outlets and platforms, there are side effects in areas not directly involved in the broadcasts. The deals increase the pressure of staff, journalists, commentators and star ex-players to conform commercially, resulting in pools of positivity, promotion and cheerleading to avoid any negativity in the broadcast. Boyle (2006, p. 125) has stated that "promoting the game is simply not what sports journalism is about", and that success on the field should shape journalistic content. This has become more of an issue with the increased commercialisation of the media (see Boyle 2006; Boyle et al. 2012; English 2013, 2016a, 2017; Rowe 2007; Schultz-Jorgensen 2005). It is important to note that praise of sportspeople and their teams is legitimate in circumstances that dictate it, but it should not occur throughout hours and weeks of broadcasts that would be better served as public-relations material.

Cheerleading and conflict of interest are likely by-products of these types of commercial arrangements. An example of the conflict of interest across owners and publications is the deal agreed by Foxtel and Channel 7 in 2018 to buy the television rights to international and domestic cricket. The size of the deal, which was double the previous agreement (Letts 2018), was major news at a time when the rights were expected to sell for lower due to the fallout from three players being suspended for using sandpaper on the ball during a Test match in South Africa. Reports in the newspaper, television, radio and online were therefore necessary and appropriate – but in most cases were glowingly positive about the deal. A story on the News Corp Australia website, *news.com.au*, said:

> Australian cricket fans are set for a brave new world in cricket coverage after Foxtel's CEO promised viewers he will "revolutionise TV cricket". In a landmark change to the Australian sporting media landscape, Foxtel and Channel 7 have seized the cricket from Channel 9 for the first time in more than 40 years.
>
> (Young & Banks 2018)

The story included an embedded video from Sky News outlining the deal. The reasons for this and other promotional coverage became clearer when, according to journalists in the survey for this book, positive stories were expected in News Corp Australia titles to support the broadcasts on partner company Fox Sports. A print journalist said the deal had compromised coverage in his newspaper. "At the start of the season, there was a lot of cross promotion, it felt like we were advertising for Fox Sports." When crowds during the domestic BBL Twenty20 competition were down on the previous year the journalist said there were discussions with editors about whether that particular story should be covered, given the negative aspect of it and the threat to the parent company's return on investment with the broadcast rights. An online journalist complained about how the advertising of Foxtel was occurring in the news section, but noted how journalists at the organisation's titles were not allowed to be critical of the company.

The following year Foxtel had a debt of more than $2 billion to parent company News Corp Australia following falling subscriptions (Kruger 2019), and there were wide-scale redundancies, including in Fox Sports, at the beginning of the Covid-19 crisis (Blackiston 2020). After the expensive entry into the international cricket rights market, there were even more reasons for the company's on-air talent to operate as promoters and spruikers of the game instead of analysing issues that might be critical to the coverage – and cost them viewers. Similar "guidelines" were occurring in Seven West Media newsrooms in Western Australia, where a supplement was being prepared each week to highlight the coverage of cricket on the television channel. One survey respondent said the only feedback from management about the extra reporting, which increased the sports journalists' workloads substantially, was there was not enough promotion of Seven. There were similar complaints by journalists about the tennis deal between Nine, which owns *The Age* and *The Sydney Morning Herald* newspapers, and the coverage of the Australian Open. *The Guardian*'s tennis correspondent, Kevin

Mitchell (2020), noted "the cheerleading television companies" involved in broadcasting the Australian Open and downplaying key issues. The positive cross-promotion highlights the increasing commercialisation of the media, which then filters through to sports journalists in newsrooms. At a time when employment is particularly precarious after rounds of redundancies and cost-cutting in major Australian newsrooms (see ACCC Digital Platforms Inquiry 2018; Doran 2020; O'Donnell et al. 2016), following the company line can ensure the journalists keep their jobs, but means they are operating in ethically dubious areas that have not been the case in previous eras. It is another example of the power of commercial factors when they are in conflict with journalistic principles.

Uniformity of content

The contemporary sports journalism field in Australia is experiencing changes through an increase in the uniformity of content being published. With such a small concentration of major print publishers, syndicated stories have expanded in line with workloads and financial restrictions in newsrooms. Previously, state-based media would have their own flavour, with shared coverage being employed when necessary, or in the national and world sections. With fewer staff, complete editions have become more uniform among sister publications, with news items coming from the same national pool of content. This has led to audiences across the country receiving similar news instead of tailored material more suited to their state. As just one example, when News Corp Australia sold *The Sunday Times* newspaper and *Perth Now* website to Seven West Media in 2018, the agreement came with a news sharing agreement that News Corp Australia content was allowed in *The West Australian* (see Ward 2016). As a result, even the smallest of the three major print-based companies in the nation uses content from a major rival, leading to more homogenous publishing across the nation. This uniformity is also a feature of online news, while television and radio broadcasts are also shared, as state-specific programs have often been considered too expensive to produce.

While *The Age* and *The Sydney Morning Herald* have had access to each other's articles, in a similar way to News Corp Australia publications, there have been changes in the amount reproduced and how these stories have been published. In the past, specialist reporters from News Corp Australia's *The Courier-Mail, The Australian, The Daily Telegraph* and the *Herald Sun* may have attended the same sporting event, and written different stories to appeal to their audiences. What is occurring now, including through the introduction of the NCA Newswire in 2020, is the same content being used – in print and online – across all publications. This has led to greater uniformity than when this issue was raised by Bourdieu (1998). Bourdieu (1998, 2005) highlighted the pressure and forces of competition were a way to ensure homogeneity, with rivals not wanting to miss out on stories and becoming more conservative, and therefore publishing the same or similar items. English (2014a) found in a newspaper study across Australia, India and the United Kingdom that there were only small amounts of exclusive material in print and online editions, with uniformity of content "a major element of contemporary sports journalism". The results from that content analysis, however, often contrasted with the perceptions of the sports journalists in the study, who insisted there were significant content differences in their publications compared with their rivals (English 2014a). Hamilton (2004) noted more than a decade ago how technology was making publishing easier and more homogeneous, a development which has increased with greater sharing of material between media outlets operating under the same parent company. The result is a lack of diversity in Australian sports journalism, despite the rise in online media titles which complement legacy publications but often rely on the same material.

Newspapers, in particular, have been losing their points of difference in the contemporary Australian sports journalism environment. While News Corp Australia tabloid titles, such as *The Daily Telegraph* and the *Herald Sun*, would previously share some content, it was rare that a story from these publications would appear in the broadsheet/quality pages of *The Australian*, the national newspaper started by Rupert Murdoch in 1964. There has been a significant shift as a result of changing management practices, workloads and softer approaches to original content. While the tag of "exclusive" still appears above stories (see Magnay & Halloran 2020 as an example), the widespread, dwindling resources have led to sports newsrooms relying on a reduced number of reporters, leaving them without the time or opportunities to search for new, newsworthy items. Of course, the days of scoops lasting from the moment a newspaper was on the streets to the evening news ended with websites and social media. But the contemporary environment, with its fractured model and wide variety of publishers, including sports organisations themselves, has led to sports journalists being unable to focus on exclusive news. Covering the day-to-day media conferences and press releases is the new bread-and-butter reporting. Bourdieu (1998, p. 6) wrote of journalists' "obsession with scoops", especially for publications closer to the market or economic pole, but in Australia it appears there is no longer this appetite – or at least it does not come across in the printed material. This adjustment has created major shifts in the field, with the control of information by sports organisations and external companies being a key factor in the absence of diverse content, along with diminishing newsroom resources.

To highlight these changes from chasing exclusive news to filling more of the newspaper with content from other publications, a one-month content analysis of bylines and tag lines in *The Australian* was conducted. This provides a snapshot of the transforming industry. In the month of October 2019, at least half of the stories in the sports section were not written by staff reporters on 16 of the 27 days *The Australian* was printed. Over the month, 46% of stories carried the bylines of the publication's staff writers. As a comparison, *The Australian* published 55.5% of articles with staff bylines in 2011, rising to 58.8% with combined staff and agency bylines (English 2014b). It is not unusual for news agency content to be utilised, since journalists cannot be everywhere, especially when covering international events, and with shrinking staff levels. However, in the eight years between samples, agency content decreased from 31.8% to 17%, with Australian Associated Press comprising 11% of stories in October 2019. The major change, at least in this snapshot, was the number of articles copied from *The Daily Telegraph*, the *Herald Sun* and other national and international sister titles. Overall, 37% of stories came from other News Corp media outlets. Sydney-based *The Daily Telegraph* (19%) and Melbourne-based the *Herald Sun* (11%) provided the most content through bylined or tag-lined articles in *The Australian* during this period, which occurred as the football codes were finishing and the summer sports were starting. Two days in particular stand out. On October 12, there were 19 stories out of 27 by staff who were not from *The Australian*. On October 10, only one of the five back-page stories – the prime sports real estate for a newspaper – was by a staff writer, and in the entire section there were three of 16 articles by staff writers. While this kind of result raises questions for audiences – why are they buying a publication that runs so few unique stories? – it also highlights the damage caused by cost-cutting in media organisations and changes in market forces and economic capital that has led to such uniformity of content.

With these types of titles, the print stories also appear on the organisation's websites – or vice versa – and with so much same or similar content being syndicated across the nation there is an absence of diverse voices and information. This is a space where websites not aligned to major print corporations can offer a point of difference, although they can also be linked to major media companies, such as ESPN's rugby and cricket sites in Australia. Despite some variety in the sports journalism field, the major players – at least in a journalistic sense – remain the television and radio companies, including the ABC and SBS, and the three parent companies controlling the biggest print and online products. The result is nationwide audiences often receiving the same sports coverage.

Former athletes as "journalists"

One of the ways broadcast companies attempt to entertain the market and boost their audience is employing ex-players as hosts, commentators and "talking heads" (see Nicholson et al. 2011; Tunstall 1995). These appointments blur the identity over what it means to be a media employee, and whether these former athletes are journalists, promoters, experts or cheerleaders who still feel part of the dressing room. There can also be confusion over the borders between broadcasts and coverage as entertainment or the delivery of public-interest information. Television is the most visible place for past players, with live broadcasts in Australia usually dominated by their comments, but they also appear in radio broadcasts, as the expert contributor, and in print and online columns, which are often "ghosted" by journalists. The athletes are hired for their special comments but can add very little other than clichés and sanitised comments for fear of upsetting "their" team. For example, Mitchell Johnson, the former Australia fast bowler, said on ABC Radio during the fourth day of the first cricket Test between Australia and Pakistan in Brisbane in 2019 that he had spoken to "the boys" – meaning the players, including former teammates – to tell them their on-field comments could be heard clearly through the microphones and were being relayed to the audience. Johnson's statements suggested the players, who were already aware of every move being recorded, should tone down their conversations so they did not get in trouble. This would protect the players but have the effect of listeners hearing less of the "real" action, and therefore covering up information. Decisions like these, which are mirrored in press conferences with current players and coaches, result in censoring or sanitising in favour of focusing on the "message" often driven by public relations or media managers to ensure no upsetting of the team or their corporate supporters.

The decision over where former athletes position themselves in their media work can be complex and have commercial ramifications. Similar decisions are made by journalists in relation to how accommodating they are with sponsors, businesses and employer connections, but former athletes are often being paid directly by these companies, creating more conflicts of interest. Comments from ex-athletes can also be blamed for upsetting the team. Instead, the role of ex-players in the media usually involves cheerleading for the home side (see Knox 2020). Early in 2020, Fox Sports' rugby union coverage was reduced, in part due to the large losses the previous year, and led to journalist, presenter and anchor Nick McArdle being dismissed. While rugby international Drew Mitchell was also let go, other former national players retained their commentary roles. McArdle was widely praised for his journalistic expertise over 13 years, but was considered expendable when compared with those with high-level playing experience. Columnist Malcolm Knox (2020) noted the qualities of past players in this instance, and how they fit within the transformed media environment. "Yet it is their biased and semi-articulate grunting, the

more inane the better, that hits hot buttons and powers the public comments pages; stupidity is the attention-grabbing commodity. The trafficking
in outrage is then mistaken for what drives ratings." This is in contrast to the
traditional approaches to journalism (see Mindich 1998; Schudson 2001),
which focus on balance, independence and critical analysis. The situation is
not only limited to rugby union or pay television services.

Australia's television cricket coverage was filled with former players
throughout the 40 years Channel 9 broadcast the game. When the rights
were split between Channel 7 and Foxtel in 2018–2019, there were more
journalists employed, including Tim Lane, Mark Howard and Alison Mitchell, but the rest of the booth was often overflowing with former players, who
were usually being supportive of the local team. At Channel 9, former Test
captains Richie Benaud and Ian Chappell viewed themselves as journalists,
with Benaud originally trained as a crime reporter. Benaud was a describer
rather than a critical watchdog-style of broadcaster. In contrast, Chappell
has been prepared to criticise players on air – including his brother Greg
when he was captain – and in his columns. Chappell will enter the press box
in between broadcasting, showing respect to journalists not applied by more
recent retired player-commentators and writes his own stories, rather than
having them "ghosted" by journalists (Lemon 2015). Chappell is also the
type of figure who can cope with criticism from the team.

But Chappell and Benaud often worked with Mark Taylor, a Test captain in the 1990s, who was also a Cricket Australia board member while
commentating – and starred in advertisements for air-conditioners in between
overs. The style of Taylor wearing two employer hats is not unusual in Australia, but it is rare to be a director of a national sporting organisation and a
commentator supposed to be sharing expert insight and opinion that often
needs to be critical. Many former players across a range of sports juggle
part-time roles. Former Australian football captain Craig Foster was a sports
news reader for SBS News, a football analyst for its other programs, and in
2019 nominated for a position of the Football Australia Board. He was also
advocating for the successful release of football player Hakeem al-Araibi
from a Thai prison. Nobody suggests that Foster, as a former player, was
soft on issues in the game in his commentary, which often contained highly
critical analysis, but it does indicate the many different shirts a former
player turned media professional can wear.

Often these conflicts of interest raise questions over where the employee's allegiance is – and it is rarely to the audience. Lemon (2015) highlighted the issues of former players dominating the commentary box during
Nine's reign, with too much jingoism, teenage-style banter, commercial
promotions and a lack of analysis by people who are actually experts. As he
wrote: "There's only room for baggy-green heroes in the box. The upshot

is part commentary, part cheer squad, and a yawning ignorance about the opposition." These comments outline the divide between former players as commentators, and former players operating as journalists. They are also important in the context of whether ex-professionals view themselves as entertainers or balanced, detached reporters of sports events and issues.

The title of "sports broadcaster" is applied for senior commentators, and more aligned with entertainment and description than sustained critical analysis. Former players usually provide the expert commentary in support of the sports broadcasters. In Australia, the most visible recent sports broadcaster has been Bruce McAveney, who has operated on television and radio to cover the Olympic Games since 1984, and athletics, swimming, AFL, horse racing and tennis. Another veteran sports broadcast is Ray Warren, "the voice of rugby league", who has been in commentary for more than 50 years in a career also including Olympic and Melbourne Cup coverage (Dalton 2017). Neither McAveney nor Warren were athletes, but AFL commentator Dennis Cometti started his career as a player. Cometti retired in 2016 and was inducted into the Sport Australia Hall of Fame for his broadcasting, which included being a sports newsreader after beginning as a radio presenter in the 1960s (Knox 2019).

In sports radio, which has been covered predominantly by the ABC, there is a host broadcaster playing a journalistic role, with an expert commentator in support, who is usually a former player. This combination occurs across a variety of sports, including cricket, rugby league, football and netball. Jim Maxwell has been the long-standing anchor of cricket coverage, while Andrew Moore is in charge of major rugby league contests. Since the start of the Super Netball competition, ex-players have been given leading roles in television broadcasts, including former Australian players Liz Ellis, who also writes a column in Fairfax Media newspapers, Cath Cox and Laura Geitz. Commentary can also come from Sue Gaudion, a former player and a coach. Again, the broadcasting is dominated by ex-athletes, who are often faced with conflicts of interest and cheerleading. This situation is prevalent throughout sports in Australia, in part due to the reliance on former players for commentary roles, but also due to the wide range of sports competing in a relatively small market. Harman (2019) notes how Lemon and Mitchell, who commentates on cricket for both television and radio in Australia, were examples of the small number who were not former professionals in broadcast boxes. In contrast to the ex-pros, who are expected to contribute tactical and technical expertise, Mitchell (in Harman 2019) said her role was "to provide the story line" and background, through developing narrative and context. In this way, she adds journalistic elements to the broadcasts.

In newspapers and online, the reporting roles are covered by journalists, with retired athletes more likely to appear in "ghosted" columns, or included as sources in stories. There are exceptions, with Tim Morrissey a former Australia basketball player who was the Head of Sport at *The Daily Telegraph* and *The Sunday Herald*, and former rugby league coach Roy Masters writing for Fairfax Media, but the combination of journalist and player is much rarer than ex-professional as commentator, broadcaster or presenter. It means the former athletes have little compulsion to undertake journalistic training or follow ethical codes – unless they chose to. This leads to blurring over their roles and their positions in the sports journalism field. In the survey, 8.3% of respondents (n = 10; eight males and two females) were former professional athletes. This included people in the positions of presenter, commentator, columnist and producer. Some of the former professional athletes said they never wanted to become journalists – one said he "always despised journalists" – and some said they still did not consider themselves journalists, even though they understood they were undertaking journalistic roles within journalism organisations.

With only a small number of former professional athletes in the study, it is difficult to generalise the results, but there are some interesting comparisons between ex-players and those who were not sports people. When asked "How important it was to be a cheerleader in your work?", 30% of former professional athletes said it was very or extremely important, compared with 3.6% of the non-professional athletes. In response to the question "How important is it to be a fan in your work?", 40% of ex-players said it was very or extremely important (compared with 31.8% of the rest of the sample). Twenty percent said it was very or extremely important to support the home team in coverage (compared with 8.3%). When asked "How important was it to satisfy athletes in their coverage?", half the former professional athletes said it was very or extremely important (compared with 10.9%), while 30% felt the same way when considering how important it was to satisfy team media managers (compared with 6.4%). In this small sample, the results outline some of the ways former players think differently than journalists on a traditional pathway into media, confirming more prevalent aspects of cheerleading, promotion and influences of commercial factors. As discussed later, these divisions were also outlined in some of the qualitative comments, with ex-players in the media seen as a threat to sports journalism.

Australian sports journalists

Sports journalists in Australia are dealing with the widespread changes in industry in their day-to-day work. The 120 sports journalists in the survey provided responses on the roles and threats in their jobs, as well as an overview of the state of the industry – and the sports journalism field. As English

(2019) has explained, there was a general sense of gloom from the respondents, with less optimism and job satisfaction due to smaller newsrooms, increased workloads, influences from sports organisations and external commercial operations, and difficulties with access to athletes and key sources. Briefly, the median age of journalists was 43, and they had spent an average of 17 years in sports journalism. Almost half were assigned to a specific round, signalling higher journalistic capital, although it is worth noting the rest could be considered as "allrounders" responsible for covering multiple sports, reflecting their workloads and skills (see English 2019). While there was job satisfaction, which was higher in newspapers, radio and news agencies, the future was not as bright for the journalists in this study compared with Nicholson et al. (2011), and there were broad concerns over the state of the industry. This included staff levels in their department, the future of sports journalism and the current state of sports journalism. Worryingly, only 28.3% of respondents said they were very satisfied or extremely satisfied with the future of journalism, while 30.8% felt the same way about the current state of journalism (see English 2019 for more details). Online journalists had the lowest levels in half of the eight topics related to satisfaction, which highlights the difficulties of a job that never really stops. Television journalists were most satisfied with job security and pay, confirming it as an area which has the most economic capital for journalists, while highlighting the precarity of work in other areas. Radio respondents were most satisfied with workload. Overall, a gloomy picture was being outlined by the sports journalists in relation to the state of the industry.

Women in Australian sports journalism

Women's sport has undergone significant shifts in professionalism and visibility over the past five years, until the stoppage caused by Covid-19. The rise of AFLW, Super Netball, the Women's Big Bash League and other sports has resulted in larger crowds, high television ratings and the expansion of female sport, at least at the professional level. Interest in women's sport has not yet transferred into females having more roles in sports newsrooms. They are still dominated by males, and sports content remains predominantly about men's sport (see English et al. 2019; Sherwood et al. 2017c). As Sherwood (2019) notes, women have not been generally welcomed into traditional sports media. Henningham (1995) has previously described sports journalism as a "man's domain" (see also Nicholson et al. 2011; Horky & Nieland 2013; Schultz-Jorgensen 2005; Sherwood et al. 2017c) and this is reflected in many components of the survey. The lack of females in sports journalism was not surprising to the respondents, including male journalists who stated there were often only one or two female journalists at major sporting matches. In this context, it is important to recognise Kelli Underwood became the first play-by-play female commentator on AFL in 2008 and *The Age* appointed Chloe Saltau as its first female sports editor in 2016. Selina Steele is a former sports editor at *The Sunday Mail* in Brisbane and at *The Sydney Morning Herald* Kathryn Wicks is a former deputy sports editor, but women in senior roles have not been a feature of Australian sports journalism.

The survey was representative in terms of gender, with 10.8% of the sample, or 13 respondents. This was slightly lower than the proportion of females in Henningham's study (1995), and higher than Nicholson et al. (2011), although neither of those surveys were representative. As noted in English (2019), it is surprising that the number of female sports journalists has not increased substantially following the rapid expansion of female professional sport. Clearly, it is still difficult for women to enter a sports newsroom. Similar to the number of former professional athletes involved in sports journalism, the proportion of females is small (n = 13), so the responses in the survey are difficult to generalise. However, there have been some noteworthy findings (see English 2019). The barrier to enter sports journalism was higher for women, with all female journalists in the survey completing a university degree (compared with 67.3% of men), and less than a third having a dedicated round (compared with 46.7% of men). Females were less likely to want to stay in sports journalism, with around two-thirds hoping to be working in the industry in five years (compared with three-quarters of men). Many respondents of both genders were not satisfied with gender equality in sports newsrooms (45.9% were either unsatisfied or a little satisfied), but females were particularly unsatisfied (m = 2.15 on a five-point scale compared with m = 2.82 for males). While females were less satisfied overall with their jobs currently, they were more satisfied with the current state of sports journalism and the future of sports journalism than their male colleagues (see English 2019).

Sports journalists (usually) like sport

Most sports journalists enter this area of the industry because they like sport. Often this feeling develops from childhood, where they start following a team and develop interests – or obsessions – over skills, tactics and statistics. As these children grow, the idea of watching sport for a job becomes enticing. The same applies to professional athletes who retire into commentary boxes. In most cases, sports journalists do their job because they love the game – or games. While their appreciation is important for knowledge and understanding of events, issues and athletes, it can also be problematic because it can lead to cheerleading or one-sided promotion.

In the survey, respondents were asked at what age they wanted to be a sports journalist. More than three-quarters had decided this was their desired career by the time they were 20. Approximately 12% wanted to work in sports journalism by age 10, and another third felt this way by 15. Almost 23% of those surveyed decided to pursue a career in sports journalism after 21. In six cases, the respondents said they did not want to work as a sports journalist – even though it was their current position. The desire to pursue a job from childhood based on a love of a sport or team can create problems or, at least, the appearance of conflicts of interest. As English (2019) found, 43 of the 120 respondents were members of a professional club. More female journalists (46.2%) were members than males (34.6%). This could include clubs in the NRL, AFL or A League. Only one respondent was a member of a professional women's club, a Sydney-based rugby league team. Membership or close links like these raise questions about the ability for the sports journalists to provide fair, balanced and independent reporting (see Boyle et al. 2012; English 2017; Garrison & Salwen 1989; Hardin 2005; McEnnis 2016; MEAA 2020; Rowe 2004). It can be especially problematic if the sports journalists are reporting on their favourite clubs or teams, which was evident in some of the responses.

At the upper end of the conflict-of-interest scale, two respondents were reporting on the teams they were awarded life membership of. Another was on the board of directors of the governing body of a sport he covered. It may be that supporting the home team through professional work is not that hard if it is the outfit a journalist grew up following and adoring. In these types of situations, a request – or pressure – from a sports organisation for more favourable coverage may be more likely to be agreed. Many journalists would dismiss this and treat the story independently, and be upset that their integrity was being questioned. Multiple respondents argued it was important *not* to be a fan or a cheerleader in their work. One journalist said he was a member of his childhood rugby league club because it meant he had greater – and quicker – access to potential news items, including many which were not released to media. However, the perception remains that sports journalists reporting on clubs that they are members of can create conflict of interest, and increase the power and impact of that particular sports organisation to influence content.

Role perceptions in Australian sport journalism

The roles of journalists in Australia have changed considerably since the rise of the internet, the impact of the Global Financial Crisis and the rapid expansion of social media. The survey was employed to gain the perceptions of those within the industry on a variety of demographic and professional topics. In the representative sample, print journalists provided the highest proportion of respondents (29%), ahead of television (28%) and radio (21%). Online-specific journalists comprised 9% of the sample, followed by magazines (8%) and news agencies (5%). In the following chapters, the predominant discussion is around the threats of commercial and sports organisations. However, it is also important in an examination of the sports journalism and sports fields to consider what journalists in contemporary newsrooms think is currently important in their work. There is a huge variety of positions in sports newsrooms, which encompass elements of traditional and modern approaches.

Reporters are still responsible for finding news, while sports editors and news producers remain in charge of deciding what is published – at least on the more "formal" programs and platforms. On social media, the decisions are more flexible, can often happen instantly and are therefore less thought out. Other positions in Australian sports journalism include production roles, such as producing, sub-editing and designing, although these are often undertaken by employees with broader duties. At *The Australian*, for example, it has not been unusual in recent years for the sports editor, Wally Mason, to write regular columns for online and print (see Mason 2020), as well as his fulfilling his role as the section head. Traditionally, the sports editor's position was about organising and managing than writing content, but times have changed. Radio journalists now do more than speak into microphones describing the play, with the need for social media and online stories. Similar multiskilling is required by television journalists, although the life of the sports presenter appears to be the most stable when compared historically. The demands on agency journalists remain high and while international newsrooms still rely predominantly on text from their journalists, reporters at Australian Associated Press were producing multimedia content for subscribers as far back as 2009. Online journalists are the most versatile and need to be able to write, report, design, plan, source photographs and edit – all under constant deadline pressure. Magazine journalists fulfil online duties in conjunction with their traditional print roles.

In the survey, each respondent was asked to name the three most important roles of sports journalism in Australia. This was to gain an understanding of whether approaches to reporting and publishing had changed, and whether more traditional techniques were still applied. After a preliminary analysis, the responses were grouped into themes that highlighted the role perceptions. The most responses related to the theme of traditional roles, which included comments on aspects of ethics, detached and independent reporting, accuracy, and educating and informing audiences. These characteristics reflect traditional views of journalism (Boyle et al. 2012; MEAA 2020; Mindich 1998; Rowe 2004; Schudson 2001). A comment explaining the approach was a print journalist saying the most important characteristics were "trust and ethics, the same across all journalism . . . You need to build that wall of trust . . . You need to behave ethically to allow people to trust you". While this has been a traditional position in journalism, it is increasingly important in a post-truth world, and one dominated by commercial and public-relations content. A magazine journalist noted the evolution of news and changes in expectations, but said in this environment it was still important to "strive to the highest ethical standards at a time when the media has changed". Ethical aspects also appeared in other comments highlighting traditional approaches to media. An online journalist stated it was an important role "to inform the Australian public in a fair manner what was happening on and off the field". Multiple respondents noted the value of educating and informing the audience while providing accurate information. These comments reflect a traditional outlook to reporting, at least in the views of the individual journalists. In a gatekeeping sense, the codes of ethics are an influence at a social institutional level, but in these responses they also indicate perceptions of their importance at an individual level (see Shoemaker & Vos 2009). It is important to recognise that the journalists' own views are impacted by the organisation in which they work (see Breed 1955). In this way, the gatekeeping selections of the sports journalists in their day-to-day work are decided by a range of factors, forces and pressures within the field.

Another major theme focused on work roles, which align with the routines level of gatekeeping. The comments dealt with the responsibilities and daily duties of staff, but could also be situated at times within the organisational space. Responses included the importance of breaking stories, but this was outlined for reasons greater than the traditional journalistic desire of generating "scoops" or exclusive material. One print reporter said in his newsroom that driving subscriptions through the website was vital and that in attracting new readers "the biggest influence is to break stories". However, another print journalist at a major organisation noted how breaking news stories did not "necessarily sell subscriptions". Articles on fantasy football teams for competitions being hosted through the website could attract more subscribers. This underlines some of the newer demands in sports newsrooms in the changing field, and a different commercial focus. Traditionally, sports newsrooms have been more about breaking stories, building an audience, beating the competition and editorial independence, rather than being compromised by the need to drive traffic through a third-party online fan competition.

Other respondents said work roles were important for sports journalism to "provide a mirror" to a nation "obsessed by sport", while some said it was essential to describe the workings of both dressing rooms and boardrooms.

In match reporting, a radio journalist said describing simply what had happened and providing reasons why a match had finished in a particular way was important. Multiple print journalists reaffirmed the value of being "a reporter, not a supporter". This links with cheerleading, which has been a traditional criticism of sports coverage, where journalists promote the home team and its players instead of providing critical analysis (see, for example, Boyle 2006; Boyle et al. 2012; English 2016a, 2017; Rowe 2007; Schultz-Jorgensen 2005). While many respondents outlined how it was critical to be objective, neutral or independent reporters than cheerleaders, there were journalists who said it was their role to "grow the game", "to promote athletes" and "to introduce people to the positivity of sport". At this point it is worth noting the comments of former England cricket coach Trevor Bayliss, an Australian, who said in comparison with England "the Australia press never criticise their own side" and "support their team" (Dobell 2019).

An overall promotional approach is in contrast to the independent, critical watchdog role played by journalists in public interest journalism, which is at the opposite pole to entertainment journalism, where sport has often sat (see ACCC 2019; Boyle 2006; Boyle & Haynes 2009; Rowe 2007; Zion et al. 2011). Alternatively, the importance of the watchdog role, which is essential in holding people and organisations to account, was outlined by multiple sports journalists in the survey. It was noticeable that this approach was not just being applied towards athletes and their on-field performances, but also to sports organisations and the wider sports community. As a radio journalist said: "Rather than being a fan of sport, hold sport to task." A print journalist linked the watchdog attitude to the roles and routines of journalists when he said it was important for sports journalism "to hold sports teams, organisations and government to account through breaking news and in-depth reporting". Scrutinising athletes and keeping sports bodies accountable was mentioned as being important by multiple respondents. Similar to the earlier comments related to ethics and detached reporting, these responses align with journalism's broader societal role of being a Fourth Estate. As an online journalist said, the most valuable role of sports journalism in Australia was to "keep power to account", therefore combining the watchdog element with traditional ethical approaches to reporting. The increased power and control of sports organisations is a pressure and influence being experienced by many sports newsrooms across the world, and has led to changes in the sports journalism and sports fields in Australia. By arguing the value of these factors, the sports journalists are outlining the continued value of exposing the truth.

Finally, a small number of responses related to diversity, particularly in women's sport and the level of reporting and broadcasting. Respondents spoke of the importance of "promoting women's sport", giving "coverage of emerging female, new and niche sports for the audience" and ensuring "a fair share of female content". They also outlined the significance of diversity in coverage through "women's sport and profiles and stories from not just traditional/men's sports". While raising the profile of women's sport continues to be essential – and a slowly growing priority for many sports organisations – the comments from these sports journalists, and the previous findings around continuing barriers of females in newsrooms (see English 2019; Sherwood 2019), indicate there is still work to be done in ensuring larger amounts of female sports coverage. This is another area in which traditional approaches to sports journalism were outlined by the nation's journalists.

An overview of threats in Australian sports journalism

While outlining the importance of roles reflects a focus on more traditional aspects of sports journalism, the journalists' perceptions highlight a range of threats to the industry based on more contemporary factors. These dangers to the present and future have emerged with the increase in power of the sports field and sports industry. The 120 respondents were asked what they considered were the major threats to Australian sports journalism, and provided up to three answers. These perceptions have been utilised to outline the dangers in an environment experiencing substantial change. The responses were coded to develop themes and three main ones emerged. The most often mentioned threat was the increased role of sports organisations in sports journalism, including providing – or in many cases blocking – access to athletes. The second theme involved the threats of commercial factors and the generally declining financial conditions of the industry. These two themes will be discussed in detail in later chapters, due to the level of threat, and the influence being exerted by external companies and organisations within sport. This is in contrast with the other most dominant theme, which related to changing media. The majority of comments applied not only to sports journalism, but other areas of journalism.

Unsurprisingly, the changing media environment has created widespread alterations. These involved shifts at macro levels, including digital transformations, to those at organisational and roles and routines levels. In some cases, the changing practices have also impacted the individual-level decisions of sports journalists in relation to ethics. In broader terms, multiple respondents highlighted issues linked with changing media structures, such as "the internet and the slow death of print journalism", in conjunction with financial issues around how to gain subscribers to support "new age" forms of journalism. The marginalisation or sidelining of sports journalism itself was also highlighted, including through a greater audience focus on the products of sports organisations, and the views of sport within media companies themselves. These wider industry threats were mentioned along with the concerns created by an increased reliance on social media, both by audiences and newsrooms. As one television journalist commented: "The advent of social media is destroying traditional conceptions of journalism." This related to the type of content desired online, its accuracy and the impact of posts on a story. A print journalist, who had earlier said his role was to tell the story accurately, stated social media was "a threat to the credibility of sports journalism" because it had affected "the attention span of people to consume news, and wanting it in a 90-character bite or headline, rather than reading what's happening". Another said social media was a "destructive force" and that errors in reporting could change the narrative of a story. An example provided was the former Australian cricketer James Faulkner (ABC 2019) posting on Instagram about his "birthday dinner with the boyfriend". This post was initially reported by some media as Faulkner being the first Australian male international cricketer to come out as gay. Respondents pointed out there had been no fact-checking on the initial post, and Faulkner had been talking about his best friend.

The rise of online and social media has led to changing views towards what have been key journalistic approaches. The accuracy of information was outlined as a threat by sports journalists due to "the proliferation of fast-food media outlets" across digital and social media that can make it difficult to understand what information is correct. As one respondent said, on social media "everyone can be a journalist, it affects credibility and accuracy". This is increasingly important in a post-truth world. Verification is a key aspect of journalism, although it is more difficult to undertake in newsrooms with fewer staff, greater workloads and more social media posts to examine from a distance. Clickbait and sensationalist news were also viewed as threats, particularly in online media, where there were claims of plagiarising and "lifting" of stories to populate websites, instead of providing appropriate attribution or undertaking original reporting. As one journalist said, the "diversification of digital media is leading to the hijacking of genuine journalists' content and hard work". Aspects such as blogging, where anyone with an opinion can claim to be a journalist or influencer, were highlighted as creating "non-qualified journalists". It was felt the lack of credibility of these content providers would then impact on traditional media through the audience's view of one-size-fits-all journalism.

This attitude can create a lack of trust from the audience that spreads throughout traditional media, where verification and fact-checking have been more ingrained as established roles. Multiple journalists noted the lack of trust in the industry as a threat. As one said simply, "fake news has leaked into sports journalism". One experienced print journalist noted that losing public trust was "far greater for newspapers than social media or digital influencers", due to the long-standing bond developed between audiences and publications. The 24-hour news cycle and push to publish first was also evident, highlighting the classic online dilemma of speed versus accuracy (see, for example, Karlsson 2011). These areas of reporting are closely linked with the ethics of the individual journalists and the organisations employing them. One respondent stated that "keeping ethical standards with the rise of online content" was a threat to sports journalism, due to the speed and conflicting demands of work. Another said in the modern media environment "the value of a fact has diminished". The environment was summed up by one radio respondent commenting: "The teeth of serious journalists have become blunted and there aren't the same questions being asked."

Multiple respondents noted the lack of newsroom resources meant there were fewer opportunities to undertake investigative journalism. However, when asked in another part of the survey how important undertaking in-depth investigations was in their work, more than half of the journalists said this was very or extremely important (m = 3.62 on a five-point scale). Examples of long-term investigations in Australian publications are rare, with an in-depth story on the finances and decline of the Australian Institute of Sport compiled by two News Corp Australia journalists being a recent example (Magnay & Halloran 2020). Previous work has also found that sports journalists have wanted to undertake more investigative work, but were often limited by resources (Hardin et al. 2009; Henningham 1995; Nicholson et al. 2011). The results in this study again link with journalists applying a traditional approach to their work, even if there are restrictions over whether they can achieve this type of aim in their own day-to-day reporting.

Broader threats to the industry were evident in comments about staffing. This included the uneven ratio between news companies and public relations firms and sports organisations, fewer opportunities for young journalists, reduced resources for those employed, and lack of advancement or wage increases. One veteran respondent noted the decline in staffing by saying when he started there were more than ten people employed in sport, but that this had been cut by more than half, including due to sub-editing outsourcing. He said there was now a greater reliance on contributors than established staff. In these conditions, journalists noted there were threats to the quality of content, and that the same information was appearing across sites. Bourdieu (1998) has argued greater competition leads to uniformity, and there were aspects of this suggested by the respondents. One said "everyone does the same thing", while another noted the high prevalence of the same agency content across seemingly every site.

Threats from within the group of sports journalists themselves were also mentioned, in relation to gender and former professional athletes. The views were occasionally conflicting on gender, but fell along gender lines. Female respondents noted a threat was how "conservative and male dominated" the industry was, and that there were "low rates of female journalism and sexist treatment of female journalists". The female sample in this study was representative, at 10.8% of respondents, but again this highlights the traditional lack of women in sports journalism, and the difficulties they can face entering sports newsrooms (see Sherwood 2019). Gender was, however, seen as a threat by one middle-aged male radio journalist, who stated there were "news editors using positive discrimination to fill newsroom positions based on sex". While no similar comments were mentioned elsewhere in the study, this statement indicates how deep-seated attitudes to gender issues and appointments can be difficult to eradicate. The employment of former professional athletes to "journalistic" roles also created resentment. This divide between those with on-field expertise and in-depth knowledge of the sports journalism profession has already been outlined. Comments from the sports journalists said a threat was "retiring sportspeople taking journalists' jobs", "former players turned journalists without any formal training" and "ex-athletes hijacking the jobs which should really be occupied by qualified and experienced journalists".

Another area where fellow sports journalists were seen as a threat occurred around cheerleading, or supporting the home team in coverage. Accusations of cheerleading have been constant across the history of sports journalism. However, it is important to state that criticism of cheerleading can be severe from those sports journalists who operate in line with traditional journalism guidelines. Multiple respondents noted the threat to journalism of cheerleaders, who would side with sports organisations to ensure coverage and access. One said "fans with typewriters" were a threat, another complained reporters were "becoming mouthpieces" and another pointed out there were "sports journalists being allowed to be a flagbearer instead of journalists". The increase in reporters being supportive of coaches and teams was noted by one respondent, with "bias and favouritism" being displayed in their work. These comments were raised in aspects of journalism ethics, identity and professionalism, and again suggest broader traditional approaches to how sports journalism in Australia should be practised.

A time of change

The Australian sports journalism field has undergone significant changes in the past two decades that have created a range of different dynamics in contemporary newsrooms. This evolution has occurred within a broader media system, but despite the difficulties it is clear that sports journalism in Australia is an important part of the industry – and a player in broader society. In this environment, the sports journalists in this study predominantly say they treat their roles seriously and apply a more traditional approach to the ethics and news-gathering processes of the job, although this can be difficult in an industry being dominated by commercial factors and sports organisations. Sports journalism in Australia is experiencing numerous threats, and there is an overall downbeat view of the state of the industry. Sports journalists are operating in a field that is often being controlled by the demands of sports organisations, is suffering due to less revenue and greater workloads, includes more homogeneity of content in its publications and broadcasts, and contains a lack of diversity. These problems in the working conditions and broader structures in sports journalism create challenges for current and future reporters.

3 The commercialisation of sports journalism

The increasing commercialisation of sport has created significant challenges for sports journalists and their publications. It is a threat that initially started to creep into content, but has become pervasive in the current media environment. While sport has been involved with commercial aspects historically, such as early stories including mentions of hospitality, entertaining and later betting (see Miller et al. 2007; Walker 2006), the commercial and financial pressures in the field of sport – and sports journalism – have become more prevalent in editorial content (English 2013, 2016c). Commercial factors and influences can take many forms, from serious financial breaches to subtle ethical transgressions, but each inclusion affects the purity of the information in a journalistic sense, and indicates the power of the external companies to infiltrate products that have traditionally been developed from a detached and independent standpoint. The regular amount of advertising or promotional content in stories highlights how sponsors and commercial interests have become a provider of content in sports pages and broadcasts – and the information does not always deal with sport. As a result, the message of the company is being promoted, rather than including only information relevant to the story.

More than a decade ago Schultz-Jorgensen (2005, p. 4) described the sports pages as "the world's best advertising agency", with the sports industry setting the agenda of coverage (see Rowe 2007; Horky & Nieland 2013). Traditionally, journalism and advertising have had an uneasy but complementary relationship – as long as advertising was kept out of editorial matters. The increased commercialisation represents both internal and external issues for news organisations. Gatekeeping decisions to allow these types of corporate inclusions, which can occur at individual, routines or organisational levels, suggest many sports journalists and publications have made concessions to the market. This shift not only reduces journalistic capital, but it contributes to a softening approach to journalistic ethics (English 2016a, 2016c). In this chapter the types of commercial factors that have become more prevalent are examined before the comments of the journalists in the surveys, which focus on commercial, ethical, cheerleading and watchdog elements, are analysed. The responses include both quantitative and qualitative elements to highlight some of the major commercial threats in Australian sports journalism.

The commercialisation of the media

As a starting point, commercialisation of the media is not new, and has also been an influence on traditional "watchdog" media (see Obijiofor & Hanusch 2011; Picard 2004). Most news organisations in Western contexts are commercial and in many of those sport's popularity has been seen as a way to improve the company's financial affairs (see Boyle 2017; Farrington et al. 2012; Nicholson et al. 2015). The concentration of media, as mentioned in Chapter 2, is also a factor along with the stories selected when the influence of profit is central (see Weedon & Wilson 2017). What has become more noticeable is the amount of inclusions in stories across media that mention commercial, advertising or company elements when they would have been ignored previously. English (2013) found commercial influences were a significant factor in the content of sports pages in both Australia and the United Kingdom, but occurred to a lesser extent in India (see also English 2016c). More than a quarter of articles in that study had at least one mention of a commercial factor, representing a shift in the focus of some media outlets, which had previously utilised publishing practices more aligned with editorial stances than corporate interference. The increase of online demands helped to create the move towards more commercial influences, and increasingly close links between sports journalism and the business elements of sport (see Schultz-Jorgensen 2005). It is also valuable to note the wider context of financial conditions of the industry, with falling revenues and reduced staff (see ACCC Digital Platforms Inquiry 2018) contributing to conflicts over journalistic and economic capital. In the new environment, journalists – and sports journalists – can apply different ethical decisions to scenarios when given a choice over whether to allow a commercial inclusion in order to stay onside with newsroom management, or protest and face the prospect of upsetting their bosses, and being more vulnerable to losing their jobs with the next rounds of cuts. Singer (2010) states the organisational restructuring of newsrooms can lead to journalists being more involved in promotion and marketing. She argues journalists have been pulled in different and often conflicting directions by new newsroom and financial structures, as well as relationships between journalists and the audience. The environment for sports journalists has altered substantially over the past decade, and news organisations are no longer always in control of coverage. However, they should not submit so readily to the market and, as will be outlined in Chapter 5, there are ways to deal with these threats that do not involve trading editorial space for advertisements.

The scale of commercial influence varies considerably, and can depend on whether the demands are made internally or externally. At the higher end of the scale is corporate collusion that results in a promotional line of content about a particular sport to boost a company's financial status, or the absence of negative stories to help an event remain popular. An example was mentioned in the previous chapter, with News Corp Australia controlling coverage of cricket through the rights deal negotiated by Foxtel and Fox Sports. Sports journalists at News Corp publications felt unable to write negative stories about cricket that were relevant to the coverage, but negative to the sport. This results in reducing journalistic capital in an effort to raise economic capital. Other moderate pressures for commercial inclusions come with advertisers or sports marketers trying to be included in editorial space, instead of during ad breaks in broadcasts, or standalone advertisements in newspapers and websites. Advertisers may request branding on the name of an international Test series, or the watch sponsor of the Sydney to Hobart Yacht Race be included in stories, photographs or strap-lines in the editorial coverage, in addition to the placement of legitimate advertisements separate to the articles. When commercial or advertising mentions are included in the editorial content it reduces the journalistic capital and purity of the articles.

Sponsors of teams and athletes are another place where commercial elements can infiltrate coverage. Journalists are often offered interviews with athletes by player managers or PR agents on the proviso they mention an aspect of the athlete's brand. *The Age* journalist Chloe Hooper (2014) reflected after an interview with Roger Federer, in which she had to ask two questions about his champagne sponsor, that "I've blown the interview. I thought it was about a game. In fact it's a story about the commercialisation of modern sport". Previously this type of request may have been dismissed and the interview arranged in a different way, but in the current market sports journalists say they will often agree to the conditions to gain an exclusive story, or beat a rival organisation (see English 2016c). While there are definitely journalistic elements in the story, the article has been diminished in a journalistic-capital sense due to the commercial tie-up and dominance of economic capital. *The Age*'s sports columnist Greg Baum (2020) wrote of the suggestions outlined by an external PR company for a 15-minute one-on-one interview with Rafael Nadal during the Australian Open: questions submitted in advance, including one about his travel insurance sponsor; a 50-word tag line of his involvement with the sponsor; an image from the sponsor; and a picture of Nadal from a press conference with the sponsor's "branded media wall" as the backdrop.

The newspaper declined the interview. As Baum wrote: "Does it matter? Yes, it does. It goes to the heart of editorial independence, and the way some think they can ride roughshod over it."

Sports journalists' travel expenses can be paid to attend matches or event launches, ensuring coverage for the organisation which may not have been given if the news outlet had to contribute, especially considering the current working and financial conditions in newsrooms. Teams or organisations have funded reporters travelling to international events such as the Giro d'Italia or World Championship swimming (see English 2016c). Domestic sporting organisations have also sent local reporters involved in the study to Big Bash League cricket fixtures, which ensure their side gets a local angle which also suits the publication's audience. In terms of roles and routines, if a reporter is rostered on they are expected to produce something each day, so if they are at an event, a story will be demanded. A condition of the funded travel may be that the athlete is photographed in a sponsor's shirt, or a tag line included either in or at the end of the story (see English 2016c). For example, an Australian Associated Press story on Ian Botham's comments before the Ashes included the line:

> The legendary all-rounder, who was speaking at the launch of his range of Australian wines at the Australian High Commission in London, said he had no sympathy for Smith, Warner and Cameron Bancroft following the sandpaper incident in Cape Town.
>
> (McCulloch 2019)

The tag line inclusion can be a way to make the commercial inclusion more transparent and less ethically grey, but still indicates sponsorship, advertising or promotional elements. Without the commercial mention, there is no interview. Traditionally, there have been other ethical issues around journalists receiving gifts, or being taken out for a meal or handed a free trip. Sometimes these activities would not appear to include any payback, but on other occasions they might involve the journalist mentioning a particular company in some way next time a relevant story appears. Some journalists, particularly those from international news agencies where the purity of information is vital, will say no to receiving any gift or inducement, no matter the value.

What is more problematic is when stories include these mentions as if they are part of the narrative. An example occurred when Australian cyclist Caleb Ewan was the subject of a wide-ranging interview in Melbourne's *Sunday Herald Sun* (Edmund 2019). The feature story covered Ewan's thoughts on his upcoming Tour de France debut, his move from an Australian-based team, and his growing family. This content gives audiences an insightful view behind the sunglasses and helmet. Towards the end of the story, in between Ewan's feelings on the Tour and the arrival of his first child, the following paragraph appears: "Ewan's blossoming talent is highlighted by the fact he is SunRice's first brand ambassador since swimmer Stephanie Rice in 2008 and the Australian company's only current sponsored athlete." Not only is the content jarring in a narrative and reporting context, but the advertising mention for a rice company highlights how sponsors and commercial interests have become a run-of-the-mill addition to the sports pages. Fewer journalists in many Western nations' newsrooms, including Australia, mean publications can be compromised by connections, or restricted access to key figures, unless they provide supportive coverage, or mentions of sponsors. It is one of the key reasons why commercial factors are a major threat to contemporary sports journalism.

There have been numerous examples when the sports pages have been infiltrated by names of external companies, as traditional and ethical approaches have weakened. English (2013) noted in a content analysis that more than a quarter of stories included commercial mentions, such as team or stadium names, or other businesses. Stadium names have become so prevalent in coverage – and among sports fans – that the sponsored title is part of the language of sport. This raises ethical issues around the routines of sports journalists. The ABC does not mention commercial stadium names in coverage, but most other organisations do in some way. Not only are these corporate companies earning free media promotion through the title, creating issues over the purity of editorial information, but they also create confusion when the short-term deals expire. Since opening in 2000, Docklands Stadium in Melbourne has been named after a finance company, a telecommunications organisation, an airline and most recently a movie franchise. A rugby league ground in Townsville was named after a dentistry business in 2019, an AFL ground in Geelong after a health insurer, and Perth Stadium sold its rights to a telecommunications company. Reporting on the business of sport is important and valid (see Masters 2020; *The Guardian* 2018), including through scrutinising the deals, but mentioning a company because it has bought the rights is giving away advertising in an editorial space.

All of these stadiums have geographical names that can be used to avoid the promotion of non-sports-story elements. In Brisbane, the rugby league and football ground Lang Park has been used since the early 1900s, but from 2003 had a financial institution title. There is no confusion when people describe it as Lang Park. Journalists and sports newsrooms can come under pressure from corporations or stadium management and there have been times when there have been threats over excluding journalists from organisations who do not mention the "official" corporate title. This situation again highlights the power sports organisations and associated bodies have – or think they have – over sports newsrooms and journalists, and how often reporters comply.

It is important to note there are cases where commercial mentions are unavoidable. The sport of cycling is an example, with teams named after sponsors, which often change each year or even mid-season. Currently Australia's most high-profile outfit, Mitchelton-Scott, is named after a winery and a bike manufacturer – and there is no other way to describe it. Some of cycling's big events in Europe, such as the Tour de France and the Giro d'Italia, started in the early 1900s as ways for newspapers to increase circulation, and have always been linked with commercial companies (see Guinness 2011; Thompson 2006). In this sport, the media have no way to report teams without promoting their brand and pedalling billboards. "Advertorials", where items are presented as legitimate stories but are really advertisements, are another commercial mention. These are prominent in some sports newspapers in relation to betting, where regular columns with punting "sources" are supplied. Similar approaches are used with straps or tickers of betting odds being run along television screens during live sport broadcasts, or crosses to betting spokespeople delivering the odds on who will score the first try, or sneeze the most during a game. It is another pervasive way for sports companies to appear legitimate – and gain recognition – through being part of sports coverage.

Ethics and commercial factors

Naming sponsors, commercial entities and advertising is often unethical. Practically, Australian journalists who are members of the Media Entertainment and Arts Alliance are bound to the Code of Ethics, while non-members can choose to follow the code (MEAA 2020). A key clause states: "Do not allow advertising or other commercial considerations to undermine accuracy, fairness or independence." This is an area in sports journalism where there is potential for conflict of interest, both in including and excluding material, ensuring access to key figures, such as athletes or officials, and developing closer relationships with sports organisations, sponsors or management teams. It is also a form of cheerleading, where support for the local team or organisation can occur to ensure smooth relations with sports organisations (see Anderson 2001; Billings et al. 2011; Boyle et al. 2012; English 2017; Garrison & Salwen 1989; Hardin 2005; Marchetti 2005; McEnnis 2016; Rowe 2004; Suggs 2016). Another clause outlines how journalists must "ensure disclosure of any direct or indirect payment made for interviews, pictures, information or stories". While in the changing sports journalism environment this would rarely involve actual payment apart from some commercial radio and television companies, organisations are often compromised – at least in comparison with traditional watchdog norms – by having to mention an athlete's sponsor, new book or whatever brand is being promoted (see English 2013, 2016c). Whether this counts as disclosure for "indirect" payment is a matter of context and how strict the interpretation is of the code, but it does involve news organisations being dominated by commercial interests to gain time with athletes in a bid for some form of exclusive news.

As Picard (2004, p. 54) states, promotion of commercial aspects "are not inherently immoral or harmful to journalism". However, he noted newspapers traditionally "placed greater emphasis on their roles as promoters of public interests and on becoming a trusted institution of society that represented the people". These comments link with those of the sports journalists who will be discussed in relation to the threat of the audience losing trust in a media publication due to the quality of information being produced. It is argued corporate mentions in editorial stories contravene interpretations of both ethical and traditional reporting guidelines. Agreeing to commercial requests can lead to better access to athletes for journalists, therefore improving their personal capital in the newsroom, and allowing them to be associated potentially with greater revenue and readership figures for their companies. But this approach goes against both ethical and traditional organisational codes, particularly in the quality titles. At the same time, in the changing environment, applying these practices can mean sports journalists keep their jobs. In this context, organising a one-on-one interview with an elite athlete on the proviso the journalist mentions their brand of shoes is considered worthwhile – and a minor ethical transgression – to enhance individual and organisational economic and cultural capital. Furthermore, if including a dentistry stadium name helps keep them away from management pressure, the sports journalists may succumb to the economic forces or organisational guidelines to ensure they remain employed. This type of gatekeeping approach also applies when there are questions about publishing – or not publishing – a story that a commercial organisation who supports either the media outlet or the sport wants hidden. Again, this type of reporting contains elements of cheerleading, where reporters boost the home team and provide coverage more suited to scrapbooks and blogs (see Anderson 2001; Billings et al. 2011; Boyle et al. 2012; English 2017; Garrison & Salwen 1989; Hardin 2005; McEnnis 2016; Rowe 2004).

Commercial factors and the field

Field theory is useful for examining how these commercial factors are affecting the sports journalism field. A major element within field theory is the forces that operate within the field, which includes agents and actors who are dominant or dominated (Bourdieu 1998). In sports journalism, the field includes journalistic forces, such as issues focused on content or organisations, but also commercial forces from the market, in terms of audiences, advertising, sponsors and sports organisations. In this space there are battles for economic and journalistic capital, with these opposing forces potentially leading to weakening of traditional journalistic and ethical approaches. It has been argued that sports journalism falls to the economic capital side of the journalistic field, with a greater focus on market, cheerleading and commercial elements than purely journalistic ones (English 2016a). Bourdieu (1998) noted publications can make concessions to the market in order to improve ratings, switching emphasis from the journalistic pole of pure reporting. In sports journalism, this can involve allowing more commercial elements into publishing, reducing the focus on traditional ethical and independent elements, and making "deals" with sports organisations or commercial interests to gain access to athletes, content or exclusive information. These forces have led to a reduction in the power of sports journalists and sports journalism in the sports field. The changing environment therefore poses significant challenges to sports journalism in relation to ethical situations, commercial factors and control.

Survey results on roles, ethics and commercial factors

In the contemporary context, it is essential to understand how the gatekeepers, or sports journalists in the newsrooms, think about aspects related to commercial factors and ethical approaches in their reporting. While the questions around specific commercial influences are crucial in this section, the comments around ethics, accuracy, traditional roles and cheerleading are also valuable in reflecting the ways they report on athletes and sports teams. These quantitative responses provide a platform for analysis that can be examined alongside qualitative comments later in the Chapter. These aspects also build on the responses of the sports journalists outlined in Chapter 2 relating to the state of the industry and the future of sports journalism.

First, the perceptions of the importance of a range of ethical aspects in the sports journalists' reporting are analysed. To examine these issues, the 120 respondents were asked to outline how important certain factors were in their work. Answer options included 1 = unimportant, 2 = a little important, 3 = somewhat important, 4 = very important and 5 = extremely important. In Table 3.1, the answers relate to ethical approaches and some roles of reporting, such as cheerleading and watchdog elements. The responses indicate the sports journalists say they treat ethical approaches as crucial. More than 90% of responses were in the very or extremely important options

Table 3.1 How important are these things in your work?

	N	Mean	Std. Deviation	Very or Extremely Important (%)	Unimportant or a Little Important (%)
Providing accurate, unbiased reports	120	4.91***	0.317	99.2	0
Being ethical	120	4.88***	0.471	97.5	2.5
Being a neutral reporter	120	4.66***	0.680	91.7	1.7
Being a detached observer	120	4.29***	0.834	82.5	17.5
Interviewing sources on the record	118	4.24***	0.844	83.1	3.39
Being critical of players	120	3.65***	1.090	55.0	12.5
Undertaking in-depth investigations	119	3.62***	1.179	53.8	16.8
Using anonymous sources	118	3.40***	1.110	42.4	16.9
Being critical of the home team	119	3.27***	1.517	52.1	29.4
Being a fan in your work	120	2.56***	1.522	32.5	51.7
Supporting the home team	118	1.75***	1.088	9.3	77.1
Feeling part of the team you are covering	120	1.66***	1.119	10.0	86.7
Being a cheerleader in your work	120	1.65***	1.034	5.8	82.5

Note: ***Independent t-tests. $p < 0.001$

for providing accurate, unbiased reports, being ethical, and being a neutral reporter. The smallest number of responses in these categories were supporting the home team, feeling part of the team you are covering, and being a cheerleader in your work. This focuses closely on cheerleading, and can indicate both ways the sports journalists provide content for their audience, but also potentially how they report to stay onside with clubs and athletes. Questions focusing on being critical of players, being critical of the home team, and undertaking in-depth investigations were considered less of a focus, with around half of the sports journalists saying these aspects were very or extremely important. In terms of other ethical roles, interviewing sources on the record was considered very or extremely important by four in five respondents, while using anonymous sources was seen as being less important overall.

The second set of topics, using the same question-and-five-answer options, focused on broader issues around sport, audiences and commercial factors (Table 3.2). There were differing responses to aspects around

Table 3.2 How important are these things in your work?

	N	Mean	Std. Deviation	Very or Extremely Important (%)	Unimportant or a Little Important (%)
Satisfying your audience	120	4.55***	0.732	91.7	1.7
Monitoring and scrutinising the sports industry	120	4.24***	0.907	80.8	5.0
Providing news that attracts the largest audience	119	3.89***	1.080	67.2	11.8
Satisfying athletes	120	2.57***	1.035	14.2	43.3
Conveying a positive image of the sports industry	120	2.53***	1.174	10.0	51.7
Satisfying your publication's advertisers	108	2.44***	1.292	23.1	56.5
Satisfying team media managers or PR staff	119	2.03***	1.025	8.4	68.1

Note: ***Independent t-tests. $p < 0.001$

newsroom-focused commercial factors. The satisfying your audience category was rated by 90% of respondents as very or extremely important, and providing news that attracts the largest audience was considered by two in three to be very or extremely important. In contrast, satisfying your publication's advertisers was considered very or extremely important by a quarter of respondents. In broader terms, the sports journalists' role of monitoring and scrutinising the sports industry was considered very or extremely important by four in five sports journalists, which links with the watchdog approach to reporting. Conveying a positive image of the sports industry was viewed as being less important, with more than half saying it was unimportant or a little important.

In this chapter, the key area for analysis focused on questions about ethical and commercial aspects around sponsors and external influences. In this series of questions respondents were asked how often they experience the following aspects in their work (Table 3.3). Answer options included 1 = never, 2 = rarely, 3 = sometimes, 4 = often and 5 = extremely often. There are some interesting differences in relation to mentioning corporate elements in stories. The commercial shift to naming stadiums after companies has resulted in almost half of the sports journalists doing this extremely often or often in their work. Alternatively, mentioning team sponsors was rated in this series of questions as occurring never or rarely by four out of five respondents. Sports journalists receiving gifts from external companies

Table 3.3 How often do you experience the following in your work?

	N	Mean	Std. Deviation	Extremely Often or Often (%)	Never or Rarely (%)
Mention corporate stadium names	119	3.20***	1.51	49.6	34.5
A reliance on metrics and audience data	120	3.03***	1.286	35.0	34.2
PR people trying to influence your stories	120	2.94***	1.079	29.2	31.7
The need to produce sensational news	120	2.15***	1.034	10.0	65.8
Receive gifts from external companies	120	1.78***	0.750	1.7	86.7
Athletes trying to influence your stories	120	1.77***	0.716	1.7	86.7
Mention sponsors of teams in stories	120	1.67***	0.929	5.0	83.3

Note: ***Independent t-tests. $p < 0.001$

did not happen frequently, although this was often said to be because com-panies rarely bothered with this strategy anymore.

The results highlight some of the forces, pressures and controls affect-ing sports journalists in Australia in the sports and sports journalism fields. They also indicate an environment in which commercial, organisational and personal factors can lead to different approaches to ethical issues. In relation to the first set of questions, which link with ethical aspects and reporting roles, the responses reflect individual journalists applying more traditional views that affect their gatekeeping, with a high level of importance placed on being ethical and reporting in a neutral, unbiased or detached way. While this indicates a more pure reporting approach, and higher journalistic capi-tal, it also suggests differences in perceptions and the agency of the actors, compared with the broader organisational and economic environment they are working in. There may also be a tendency to say this is what they would do, rather than what they are able to do in a newsroom setting, or what the organisation is capable of achieving in the macro environment. Tandoc et al. (2013) are among those who have noted differences in journalists' role perceptions and their enactments. An example is the responses to the importance of in-depth investigations, with many sports journalists indicat-ing they wanted to do more investigations, but did not have the resources to undertake them themselves. While cheerleading, supporting the home team and feeling part of the team were rated as the least important of the topics in that series of questions, previous research into content has shown that stories are likely to include elements of cheerleading and reporting focused on the home team (English 2017). Comments from the sports journalists themselves in Chapter 2 have also highlighted how some see their role as being "promoters" of the game. Being critical in their reporting, and there-fore employing a watchdog role, was not seen as important for many of the sports journalists, which has been reflected in previous research and other areas of the industry (see Boyle 2017; English 2016a). Again, however, this was outlined as being a crucial role of reporting by many in the qualitative questions of the survey in Chapter 2.

The second list of factors, including broader issues around sport, audi-ences and commercial aspects, also indicated that newsroom-related per-ceptions tended to fall in line with traditional journalistic approaches. Satisfying audiences and providing news attracting the largest audience were considered more important to the respondents than satisfying the pub-lication's advertisers. However, almost a quarter of the sports journalists said this advertising aspect was very or extremely important, reflecting changes in the industry focus and difficulties in gaining and maintaining economic capital. The broader role of journalism's watchdog and ethical approaches to sport produced answers that supported traditional views on both scrutiny and promotion of the sports industry respectively. This also links with the qualitative responses from Chapter 2 in relation to key journalistic roles. However, 10% of respondents thought it very or extremely important to convey a positive image of the sports industry, which aligns with the promotional view of sports journalism (see Boyle 2017; Schultz-Jorgensen 2005) and the earlier comments of some of the sports journalists.

Finally, the results focusing on how often ethical and commercial aspects occurred around sponsors and external influences produced some conflicting data. Naming of stadiums happened much more often than mentioning team sponsors, according to the journalists. This is a contradictory result given many teams are "named" after sponsors in media releases, such as the Wallabies rugby union team's affiliation with an Australian airline or the Queensland Reds' association with a domestic bank, yet the sports journalists say these companies do not get their descriptions in stories, while stadium names do. Previous research, as well as media examples, has shown content often includes commercial inclusions, including sponsor mentions for setting up "exclusive" interviews (see Baum 2020; Edmund 2019; English 2013, 2016c; Hooper 2014; McCulloch 2019). The naming of stadiums can be more complex, with companies buying rights to the "official" title, although as stated previously most venues were named around geographic locations originally.

Sports journalists' perceptions on commercial conditions

Commercial factors were considered a major issue when examining the concerns outlined by the sports journalists in the qualitative questions. As mentioned in Chapter 2, the respondents were asked to name three key threats in the industry. Commercial factors and the generally declining financial conditions were a major theme. Combined with the results mentioned earlier, the comments in this section confirm the seriousness of the impact and influence related to resources, and indicate the restricted environment is having an effect on the roles, routines and content produced by a smaller number of staff in Australian sports newsrooms.

A lack of resources and budget cutting was a common issue along with problems with the business model of journalism as a whole. As one online sports journalist said, a threat was "executives understanding they can't go back to how it used to be, so they were just doing the same with less resources". A lack of money was a regular complaint that had many repercussions. Journalists talked about the redundancies of colleagues leaving remaining staff "stretched thin, doing a lot more with a lot less". This led to more mistakes and coverage that was not as in-depth as previously. One online journalist noted how tight deadlines caused a lack of accuracy that meant journalists were "first rather than right". Karlsson (2011) has outlined these problems in online news, and it is evident the situation has not improved now fewer staff are being employed. In a commercial sense, the media has always focused on profit, but the quality of content has also been a key consideration in most newsrooms.

A broader threat, according to an online reporter, was the "lack of independence and monopolies" in the Australian media. This comment links with the previously noted conflicts of News Corp Australia controlling content across pay television, newspapers and websites. Another example of the influence of this parent company was an item in a diary-style column in Brisbane's *The Sunday Mail* headlined "Going all out for Kayo" (Davis 2020). The story was about a rugby league advertisement for streaming service Kayo, involving a player from the Brisbane Broncos. The newspaper, streaming service and rugby league team are all owned by News Corp Australia, as well as advertising content being included in editorial space, highlighting the cross-promotion and ethical issues. A news agency journalist noted that if media companies closed – or continued to merge in the case of Fairfax Media and Nine – it "narrows" the number of sources providing news. Australia's media ownership is already heavily centralised, which creates problems with homogenous content and following the companies' profit agenda (see Weedon & Wilson 2017). The agency reporter stated when big organisations merge, the same stories are printed everywhere and the result is news that is "lacking credibility". It also leads to uniformity of content (see Bourdieu 1998).

Rights deals developed by media organisations, particularly in television and radio, were also outlined as a threat. Sport is a rare area in journalism in that its organisations can pay for access to broadcast matches, with record-breaking rights deals being completed in recent years (ABC 2015; Fox Sports 2015; Letts 2018). The sports journalists were concerned that these agreements meant restrictions were imposed on other media by rights holders. For example, the demands of a host broadcaster can limit the availability of key sources and athletes to other media attending a match. On-field interviews could be granted to rights holders, while other players or coaches who are less newsworthy to the stories of the day appear at the media conferences. By buying rights, organisations effectively purchase access to players, which highlights the benefits of economic capital. In the AFL Women's competition players must be available for interviews with the host broadcaster before and after training (AFLW 2019), with similar arrangements in other sports. With the extra financial power comes exclusive content, but it can come at a cost to journalistic capital and pure reporting.

The reluctance of the audience to pay for sports journalism was also mentioned as an issue contributing to the financial state of the industry. However, the rise of data and the value of subscriptions, particularly to online publications, has meant there is now more feedback available to journalists. It also results in newsrooms targeting particular markets in the hope of gaining more subscribers. One senior print journalist said his organisation was experimenting with greater coverage of hockey, which was seen as a middle-class sport, in the hope it would lift the audience base. Journalists, too, noted how the lack of resources meant they could not cover as many events as previously, and there were greater restrictions on travel. This has been occurring more regularly in recent times, including during events such as the 2019 Rugby World Cup, where News Corp Australia shared content again throughout their broadsheet and tabloid publications. However, it is also happening domestically, and even more now with the introduction of its NCA Newswire, which again leads to more uniformity of content (see Bourdieu 1998). As a senior print journalist at a major tabloid newspaper said: "I now cover rugby league off tv and watch press conferences on NRL. com.au." It shows that sports organisation websites, which are rivals of news organisations, are being utilised for content even though they are competitors because the material can be viewed cheaply and easily. It was also mentioned how reduced travel budgets restricted the journalists' ability to gain access to athletes because they were not "on the ground" at events to get closer to key sources. This is a major factor that will be discussed in detail in the next chapter. The lack of resources was also affecting investigative journalism, which many journalists in the survey thought was important, but there were limited examples of it occurring in practice (see Magnay & Halloran 2020 as an exception). Sponsors protecting their brand and broadcast rights deals were also seen as a commercial threat by journalists.

Commercial concerns

The results in this section highlight some significant concerns over the influence of commercial factors in Australian sports journalism. This is particularly problematic because it indicates a lack of editorial independence and an increasingly lenient attitude to aspects that would have been ignored previously. It needs to be restated that journalists and organisations are operating in precarious times, and that if mentioning a commercial aspect ensures a journalist keeps their job, it may not be viewed as a major ethical issue. But the results highlight deeper concerns between journalists, newsrooms, sports organisations and sports business. When Schultz-Jorgensen (2005, p. 4) wrote the sports pages were "the world's best advertising agency" the comments applied generally to publications promoting particular sports and avoiding critical topics. Schultz-Jorgensen (2005) argued that a global partnership between the sports industry and sports journalism had formed, suggesting "some deeply problematic consequences for sports journalism" due to the sports industry setting the agenda for the coverage (see also Rowe

2007; Horky & Nieland 2013). Over the past 15 years the situation, at least in Australia, has developed into less of a partnership and more one of sports journalism being dominated by commercial interests and the control of sports organisations. In the context of Bourdieu's field theory (1984, 1998), these developments reflect sports journalism's much lower levels of economic and journalistic capital, and a dominated place in the contemporary sports field.

The weakening economic capital of newsrooms, particularly in Western nations since the GFC and through the development of online and social media, has resulted in fewer staff and less advertising revenue. Subsequently, the lack of economic capital has created the potential for a considerable loosening of ethical bonds and newsroom approaches that threaten the purity of the published information. Audience metrics have increased in value, with individual journalists capable of knowing not only how many hits their stories are attracting, but also the number of online subscriptions their work is generating. This can change the focus to entertainment topics instead of public service issues that inform and educate. In the current context, the conditions can leave journalists scrambling for any advantage and, while this study is not suggesting they will use any means to get stories, published content indicates they are applying approaches not previously utilised regularly in a bid to attract audiences and hold on to their jobs.

One of the ways has been a greater acceptance of commercial elements in stories, which raises ethical and conflict-of-interest points for discussion around whether this counts as disclosure and "indirect payment". Overall, these examples outline how some publications have made concessions to the market in an effort to retain some form of capital and to continue to be players in the field (Bourdieu 1998). But the rise in commercial mentions in content (see English 2013, 2016c), despite what the journalists in this study have outlined, provides another example of how sports journalism is being dominated in the sports and sports journalism fields by commercial operations and sports organisations. Given the limited economic capital of journalism in many Western nations, the choice in some newsrooms appears to have been made to submit to this force in the hope of preserving a place in the field.

4 Sports organisations and media dominance

The power and financial growth of sport has provided professional sports organisations, clubs and teams with more control in the sports field. With their expanding economic capital – at least until the major setbacks delivered by the Covid-19 crisis – organisations in major and niche sports have been able to determine the agenda, fixture lists, players and personnel, media rights and, in many cases, influence what appears in publications. While sports organisations' financial positions have been strengthened by record-breaking rights deals over the past decade, including in Australia (ABC 2015; Fox Sports 2015; Letts 2018), the balance sheets of journalistic organisations have been generally in decline. This has led to a repositioning of key elements of the sports and sports journalism fields. In this battle for capital, sports organisations have gained more control over the messages being published and broadcast to the point where it can be difficult for sports journalists to do their jobs properly, at least in comparison with traditional and pure approaches to journalism of honesty, independence and ethics. The dominance of sports organisations is a major threat to sports journalism, both now and into the future. In this study, the most common threat outlined by sports journalists was the increased role and power of sports organisations.

The rising commercial and corporate culture of sport has led to many changes, including alterations in the media model, such as how information is delivered, and the rise of digital media. Previously large sports organisations would rely on the media to spread their message and work together. Through the transformation of digital media, they now deliver the information themselves via in-house media developed by staff, who can be either public relations officials or commercial or club "journalists", providing favourable – or at least sympathetic – coverage whatever the "real" story. The rise of sports organisations is closely linked with the threats provided by the influence of commercial factors mentioned in the previous chapter. Sports organisations now exercise their power through control and restricted access of the media, which is detrimental to sports journalism and their audiences. Another area of the altered landscape that has had a considerable impact on sports journalists is an increased focus on media management, which has created more sanitised, promotional content in the public domain. Again, these changes, which are outlined by the survey respondents, threaten the traditional role played by sports journalists, whose public-service duty is to inform the public of the workings of clubs and teams. With sports organisations holding so much power, they can often control the output of sports journalists who, in effect, may have to toe the "company" line to be able to do their job in a newsworthy way. There can also be restricted access to media conferences or staged events when journalists are critical of an organisation or its athletes. Until the Covid-19 cutbacks and stand-downs, there had been an expansion of communications, PR and in-house media roles in many sporting bodies. This has created traditional journalistic titles competing with the "media" of sports organisations themselves. Athletes also publish on their own dedicated platforms, including social media, which bypass traditional media. The power of the sporting body can therefore encourage sports journalists to follow the team message, instead of fulfilling the role of a more critical and independent reporter. The results are a less informed audience that receives predominantly positive stories. The changing environment, including the influential commercial factors already outlined, poses significant challenges to sports journalism in relation to ethics, independent access and control.

The rise of sports organisations

Sports organisations may be not-for-profit and aim to govern in the best interests of the game but are commercial entities, particularly when it comes to negotiating rich broadcast rights deals for major sports (see ABC 2015; Fox Sports 2015; Letts 2018). Whereas once these larger organisations relied on and worked together with newsrooms to publicise contests (see McChesney 1989; Mirer 2019; Sherwood et al. 2017a), these bodies now control much of the media and access themselves due to the economic power they generate. The substantial expansion by commercial and sports operations means they are now dominating the field instead of media organisations, including through control, influence and pressure. In many ways, the sporting bodies have cut off their alliances with their former partners – unless they are rights holders – seeing the media more as a nuisance who will disrupt their message by applying critical questions and thought to issues or comments. These challenges mean sports journalism is experiencing major reductions in both economic and journalistic capital. As mentioned previously, the sports pages have been described as "the world's best advertising agency", and the sports industry has been responsible for setting the agenda of coverage (see Horky & Nieland 2013; Rowe 2007). However, the situation has changed considerably in the past decade. An increased focus on media management has created more bland, promotional content in sports news, which is in addition to the rise of in-house media (see Jackson 2019; Mirer 2018). As a result, the influence of a sporting organisation can encourage sports journalists to follow the team's line and act as cheerleaders, instead of fulfilling the role of a more critical reporter (see Boyle et al. 2012; Garrison & Salwen 1989; Hardin 2005; Marchetti 2005; McEnnis 2016; Rowe 2004) to retain access and favour. With fewer journalists in contemporary Australian newsrooms, and the desperation to maintain audience figures, reporters and their publications can be compromised in their ethical and gatekeeping decisions.

A major commercial complication in the field is traditional titles are competing with the "media" provided by sports organisations themselves, or athletes publishing on their own platforms. In-house publications, such as afl.com.au and nrl.com.au, are rivals to media outlets but have the benefit of the overarching body controlling the information, the sources and what is ultimately published. Complaints in the survey, based around the question of major threats to the industry, included that after a media opportunity the video of the conference would be published on the sports organisation's website immediately – well before the journalists were back in the newsroom attempting to produce their own material. News outlets were being beaten to publishing by the sports organisations, which increased their control over breaking news. These sites also often produce one-sided promotional pieces without the scrutiny placed on them by an independent journalistic approach. The content providers know they have to follow the party line, but many of those who have worked for newsrooms before entering the corporate arena still identify as journalists (Mirer 2019). This is despite problems with ethics, independence and omitting relevant content (see MEAA 2020). In the survey comments, respondents from the major metropolitan newsrooms questioned the journalistic identity of those working for in-house media. As a print rugby league writer said, "They say they are journalists" but are "mouthpieces" for their organisations.

Writing in the United States, Mirer (2019, p. 185) notes the rush of sports into media production and how their websites have been turned into news operations. In journalism this has resulted in "loosened professional control over news" and a situation that has "displaced sports journalists from the central position they occupied" previously (Mirer 2019, p. 185). One respondent in the current study noted that in the United Kingdom there was a lesser focus on sports organisations producing their own content. As the journalist said: "There's nothing like the same push in England – like in Australia with afl.com.au or cricket.com.au. The press is broader and not the same. The FA is not setting up its own news arm." In Australia, Sherwood et al. (2017a) found public relations staff at an AFL club had changed their approach to their own distribution channels instead of relying on mainstream media to disseminate information. This included the media staff developing and communicating "'sensitive' stories in which they wished to control the narrative" (Sherwood et al. 2017a, p. 527). They conclude these changes have considerable implications for sports journalism, with the sporting bodies' media changing the "once symbiotic relationship between sport and media", and limiting sports journalists' access to sources. They also found media was limited by the material provided by clubs, who were "assuming more control over the media agenda by actively framing their information subsidies and then controlling access to those information subsidies" (Sherwood et al. 2017b). As they argue, this is problematic for sports journalists, whose primary relationship is now with club media staff instead of players, coaches or officials. It means journalists are "left with very few alternatives other than to accept the version of reality presented to them by sport organisations" (Sherwood et al. 2017b, p. 1005; see also Hutchins & Boyle 2017). With verification or alternative voices increasingly difficult to obtain, journalists often have to accept the club's line on a story or issue. As Sherwood et al. (2017b, p. 1005) conclude: "It would appear that, in this Australian case, sport journalism has been complicit in ceding control of the sport media agenda to professional sport organisations." Writing about AFL coverage and the newspapers' reliance on material from clubs, Jackson (2019) was also critical of the current approach of the media, and questioned "why a burgeoning football media machine had seemingly given up on offering the paying customer a worthwhile read". These decisions provide more signs of the changing levels of capital in the sports field, where sports journalism is now being dominated by sporting bodies, instead of being in control like it was in previous eras.

In sections of sports media, there are also requirements to satisfy the sports organisation selling and hosting the matches for broadcasting. These deals are not limited to Australia, with a senior radio broadcaster saying that in India, where the national cricket board controls content, a commentator's contract outlines what aspects cannot be criticised. In Australia, a senior radio journalist said a normal broadcasting agreement outlined how commentators and presenters were not to criticise elements related to those hosting the broadcast (see also Mitchell 2020). These agreements – and external gatekeeping elements – impact on what can and cannot be reported. As mentioned in Chapter 2, these issues have been a prominent factor in Australian media, including with deals between News Corp Australia, Foxtel and Cricket Australia. After the allrounder Marcus Stoinis was fined for a homophobic slur towards an opponent during a domestic Twenty20 match, there were discussions over whether a journalist operating as a host broadcaster "boundary rider" could raise the same issues as those that occur more critically in a press conference (Lalor 2020b). The debate misses a key point, and indicates players and sports organisations see journalists as either supporters or opponents. If a reporter is operating as a journalist, they should be able to ask a question – critical or positive – whatever the location. Sadly for the traditional approach to journalism, these commercial complexities are now a feature of discussions around contemporary sports coverage.

The sports field also involves "media" set up by players or managers themselves, through online and social media. This includes the Australian publication *PlayersVoice*, which changed in 2019 to *AthletesVoice*. Sites like these offer athletes a safe place to publish their stories – often through their agents – without the critical lens or choices over subject selection that journalists make through their gatekeeping. *AthletesVoice* (2020) was established with support of elite athletes who were finding "dissatisfaction with the negativity of coverage in some traditional media outlets". So, knowing that the article will be positive and copy-approved, athletes are more likely to tell their story than being open and engaging at media conferences where they cannot determine how their comments appear. It is another example of the combination of commercial factors and sports organisations limiting information and making it harder for sports journalists to report because they no longer have access to these primary sources, which are viewed as high-capital inclusions in stories by newsrooms and audiences. In this environment, sports journalists and their publications are experiencing a reduction in journalistic and economic capital, which is affecting their ability to produce material that informs, educates and entertains. Instead, the influence of sports organisations means these non-journalistic bodies are dominating the field. Sports journalists and their newsrooms are battling to stay in the game.

Why sports journalists need access

Journalists across all subfields require sources to report effectively. In sport, interviews are a staple of news and feature content, but can also inform analysis and comment pieces. The thoughts of athletes, coaches and officials about themselves, teammates, matches, injuries, tactics or trivialities form the base of coverage not focused specifically on match reporting. Preview stories rely on comments about the upcoming contest, and can sometimes occur months ahead of the fixture (see Glenn McGrath's regular Ashes predictions). After games the reflections of players and coaches on significant moments are central to the stories, as well as for updates on hamstrings and heels. One of the key roles of journalists is to report information that informs audiences on what has occurred in a particular scenario and then to ensure the details are correct.

Feature stories, either as wide-ranging interviews or articles focusing on topical or historical issues, usually require contact with key sources, and provide more background and human interest. Without access to the subject, or with access to ones who stonewall or spout corporate lines, the stories are not only less interesting, but less truthful. With space in TV and radio bulletins and newspaper and online sports sections to fill, sports newsrooms have to produce something each day. When there is limited access to talent, the fare served up from sanitised media conferences fills the air. Media managers and PR agents know newsroom gatekeepers have to allow some content through, and the sports organisation gatekeepers try to keep anything controversial out. By controlling the information and access, sports organisations can heavily influence the news cycle, limiting information for audiences and the public, and preventing journalists from highlighting more newsworthy elements. McEnnis (2019, p. 88) notes how public relations is "a heavily constraining factor" on the ability of sports journalists to gain access to athletes and "compromises their autonomy in being able to act freely in the pursuit of stories" (see also Sherwood et al. 2017a). In Hutchins and Boyle (2017, p. 505), a sports journalist describes communications and public relations staff as "media prevention officers". Suggs (2016) recognises the dangers of organisations placing restrictions on journalists, creating issues for stories of public interest. Another significant problem, particularly in the current financial climate, is that without quality content and access to high-profile athletes, officials and events, audiences will decline, which further reduces economic capital. Journalists and newsrooms can make gatekeeping decisions to include content from sports organisations that is unfiltered and not assessed with a critical eye. The result is that in many publications there is now more of an entertainment focus based on limited information instead of a public-service approach to news.

Ethically, journalists aim to attribute information to its source (MEAA 2020), but unattributed content is included in many stories, as it is in other areas of journalism, such as politics. There are many good reasons why an interviewee may request anonymity, including protecting themselves or their team, or not wanting to jeopardise their position. However, no attribution is often a condition of quoting a media manager so they are not named, or are described generically instead as a spokesman/woman or team official. This can be because, they claim, the advisor is speaking on behalf of the organisation, official or athlete, and not themselves. In many sports there have been an expanding number of media advisors dealing with requests for comment, who double as spokespeople for clubs (see Sherwood et al.

2017b). This unattributed information can lead to questions over the credibility of the comments. Workloads and staffing can also contribute to this agreement, with unattributed content from spokespeople easier to find on a busy day than a one-on-one with an athlete in between training and other commitments.

Other ethical issues in relation to content provided by sports organisations focus on the MEAA (2020) clause on reporting and interpreting honestly. This includes "striving for accuracy, fairness and disclosure of all essential facts. Do not suppress relevant available facts" (MEAA 2020). When stories are controversial or likely to paint an athlete, club or sponsor in a negative light, sports organisations can attempt to pressure the reporters into not running them. This could include a deal to gain access to another interview target, or result in a reporter being sidelined from press conferences or, in more extreme cases, having their accreditation revoked for critical reporting. This occurred in South Africa in 2019 during a dispute between Cricket South Africa and journalists reporting on board decisions (*Wisden* 2019). A print journalist in the survey said he was currently prevented from one-on-one interviews with competitors in an Olympic sport due to coverage seen by that organisation as negative. Instead, he was limited to general media conferences along with every other journalist. Similar to the commercial influences outlined in the previous chapter, under-pressure journalists could be tempted to take what they can get, in terms of information or access, to produce a story rather than missing out. Independence and fairness in reporting can also be an issue, along with cheerleading and bias, particularly when sports journalists are members of sporting clubs they are reporting on (see Boyle et al. 2012; English 2017; Hardin 2005; MEAA 2020). There are often times when journalists have to weigh up how to keep sources close and the demands of breaking stories, which Weedon and Wilson (2017) argue is another ethical matter. The changing practices of the field, with sports organisations gaining more control due to increased economic capital, has led to media managers and sports organisations having a greater influence, with power to attempt to change what is included in stories, and what is left out. This is impacting on the quality of content being produced by sports journalists, and leading to audiences who are less informed about athletes, clubs and sporting teams.

Changes to media access

Media access used to be much more simple, and led to greater interactions – and understanding – between athletes and sports journalists. Journalists themselves could organise the interview by calling the source at home, work or on their mobile. The team manager might help organise end-of-match media conferences, but they were relatively casual affairs, free of sponsors' branding apart from a cap or t-shirt, and held outside dressing rooms or wherever space was available. In reality, they were only attended by a handful of journalists working for major print or broadcast media. Scyld Berry (2020), a journalist who spent 43 years touring with the England cricket team, noted how when he started players and reporters would discuss the game in a bar after play each night, in an off-the-record capacity with "complete trust" (see also Jackson 2019). He wrote how when they travelled "players and press were a single party", but noted the environment changed when Ian Botham, the star of the 1980s, became a tabloid columnist and a target to other publications. Berry wrote the relationship between players and media is now "them and us". An experienced Australian print reporter, who has worked across multiple elite sports, said in the survey "the relationships between mainstream media and players has never been further apart". What this distance can provide, however, is a detachment from sources that allows for greater independence in reporting.

Similar shifts in Australian journalism can be traced to the rise of legspinner Shane Warne in the 1990s, who was an A-list talent on and off the field, with after-hours incidents involving passing information to bookmakers, being banned for using a diuretic, having extra-marital affairs and smoking. As noted by Coward (2015), interviews back then could be held in hotel rooms – and there was no need for security or PR agents to be called. Now, sports columnist Greg Baum (2020) notes: "All sports ration out their stars to media now. At one level, that is only to be expected: demand is enormous." While these limits occur across the world, there are exceptions. In the United States, locker room access for journalists has been standard, at least until the playing lockout caused by Covid-19 (Curtis 2020). Irish sportswriter Paul Kimmage (2020) wrote that Rory McIlroy, the four-time major golf winner, has allowed him to be interviewed in his bedroom and that "no question was off limits" during two interviews over three years – and there was no plugging of sponsors or products.

In Australia, media managers for sports organisations became more popular in the 1990s and, at that time, were more facilitators than blockers, organising interview times, or passing on phone numbers. It was rare that a request was dismissed, although it is important to note, as Baum (2020) wrote, this was before the proliferation of online and social media resulting in expanding publications and increased demand. Media managers started travelling with teams and, like advisors in politics, there were soon small armies of corporate staff in media rooms offering spin, deflections or dead bats. *The Age* sports journalist Martin Blake (2012) wrote about the benefits of being able to talk more freely with athletes, on and off the record, during a tour.

Generally you stayed at the same hotels and went to the same bars, so if a player had an issue with you, they had every chance to take it up. It was a better way – nowadays there would be some spin merchant brokering a deal.

There are dangers in journalists being embedded in the team, or too close to players, and becoming cheerleaders instead of reporters. But journalists often make the decision that it is better to have some link than be on the outer.

The situation in sports media relations has changed so dramatically that being able to ring an athlete, without first going through a media manager, is increasingly rare in major sports for all but the most well-connected journalists. Now enquiries go through the media teams, and a likely result is being told of an upcoming media conference. A radio journalist in the current study summed up the situation by complaining about "the lack of access to individual athletes because of clubs controlling media opportunities". Staged conferences are a daily staple in major sports, but rarely deal in detail with the issue of the moment. Controversial topics are often covered through the organisation's in-house publications to ensure smooth, uncritical or sympathetic treatment. Most worryingly, the statements are copied across media platforms, especially online, as newsroom staff turn around the press releases quickly before switching attention to the next story.

Crucially, media managers or advisors or heads of communication often have a journalistic background. At first, this may offer sports journalists encouragement in that the PR agent understands their role and interview requests will gain a fair hearing. However, the former journalists know all the tricks, having turned from the poachers of sensitive information themselves to the gatekeepers who block questions and float the corporate line. For example, Cricket New South Wales has Malcolm Conn, a former Walkley Award-winning journalist, in charge of its communications (The Walkley Foundation 1999) while Cricket Australia's Head of Communications is Alex Brown, who previously held senior roles at News Corp Australia, Fox Sports and Fairfax Media. Both were hugely respected for their news-gathering abilities – including investigating and gaining unauthorised exclusives from the organisations they currently work for – but now represent those corporate views.

Facing former colleagues in sports organisations can make the role of the sports journalist even more difficult in gaining access and information. This is more challenging with the staffing and workload conditions in many contemporary newsrooms. It is important to note media managers can be helpful in providing information quickly and easily. However, the view of sports journalists was summed up by a radio journalist in the survey who said it was a challenge "asking the tough questions and getting railroaded by media managers and former contacts", who would stop difficult questions, or prevent follow-ups. The journalist said this approach "prevents journalism from fully being realised". A senior magazine writer described a change in gatekeeping as a result of the transformation of media. This involved "the increasing difficulty of gaining access to clubs and athletes at all levels", and the "proliferation of online story platforms enabling athletes to speak directly to fans". The gatekeeping shifts have created many challenges for sports journalists, who now rely predominantly on "official" figures for access, and may change their own gatekeeping decisions to ensure new, unique or non-media conference content in their stories.

While the traditional conditions on access and interviews placed more demands on players – or their managers – it meant that they were interacting with sports journalists more often. Disagreements could be raised with previous stories or issues (see Blake 2012), or background information provided (see Jackson 2019), helping the sports journalist achieve more accurate and informed coverage. In contemporary sports journalism, these types of briefings are delivered by the media managers themselves, and are therefore tainted and restricted by the position of the organisation. Previously, the character of the athletes themselves could also emerge, compared with the current interactions which often involve bland offerings that have been workshopped beforehand with media management staff. The rise of sports organisations has created an environment in which supporters may be happy with uncritical content, but one in which the public is often left not knowing the full story, and not having issues, results or players examined in critical ways. Jackson (2019, pp. 20–21) notes how current coaches are "tight-lipped and sealed off" at media conferences and it is "hard to escape the feeling they're giving more exposure to the logos of the club's corporate backers than to their honest thoughts on the game".

Major sports are masters at this type of media management, but sports looking to gain a greater market share even place restrictions on their players around media interactions. Super Netball athletes are limited to how many media appearances they can do, and a clause in the AFL Women's collective bargaining agreement states players will not be directed to do media interviews in their free time (AFLW 2019). Journalists involved in cycling have also noted recently a change from open access to more restrictions and all requests funnelling through media advisors. In employing media managers – and different levels of communication and public relations staff – the scene has altered from a space where asking for interviews, information or verification was manageable for sports journalists, to one that is increasingly difficult – and getting worse according to the survey respondents. While the players may appear to benefit through fewer public interactions with sports journalists – and less scrutiny of their comments and actions – it does stop them from gaining greater understanding about the media, and prevents the developing of relationships that may actually lead to better reporting. As shown in the past, it could also generate less of a "them and us" schism (see Berry 2020).

The popularity of recent documentaries *The Last Dance*, about Michael Jordan and the Chicago Bulls' dynasty, and *The Test*, which covered Australia's cricket team after its sandpaper suspensions, displayed some of the benefits of "open" athletes. However, it is essential to recognise key players in both productions could approve or reject content. The transparency impressed Hawthorn player Chad Wingard (2020) who said: "I would love to see AFL players showing that kind of personality when they're being interviewed and I loved how the documentary did a great job of humanising the players, while also allowing them to speak their minds." Wingard's response – appearing on his club's website – also indicated how the players do not understand the role of sports journalism.

> The part of the media I don't like is when they cut out a quote from an interview and it's not in context with what you've said throughout the entire press conference and it ends up on the back page of the paper. It portrays such a picture of yourself and I think that's what the players are worried about. They'd rather have as much control as they can over their personal image and what they believe in and stand for. We've all got personal brands to look after.

This player's response outlines the differences between sports organisations and athletes seeking control, and sports journalists pursuing truthful information. The power of sporting bodies in ensuring their message is spread indicates a weakening of power and capital in sports journalism, and causes audiences to be less informed about matters in the public interest. Instead readers, viewers and listeners are receiving more one-sided accounts brimming with sports-organisation spin, bias and cheerleading.

It is essential to recognise that the number of news organisations have expanded, particularly online, and various requests are put in for interviews with key figures from across media. Exclusive interviews are therefore increasingly difficult – and may rely on some type of commercial tie-up (see Baum 2020; Hooper 2014). However, specific organisations and journalists have always been prioritised by athletes and clubs. According to a small number of journalists in the study this still occurs, but only in major organisations. Based on many comments across mediums, this has changed considerably and all organisations at times have problems and concerns with the amount of access being granted. This will be discussed in detail in the interview responses later in this chapter, but highlights the impact the sports organisation restrictions are having on content and quality of the information being produced.

Survey results on sports organisation factors

To gain an understanding of the issues sports journalists face in relation to sports organisations, they were asked a range of questions on a five-point scale about their interactions and approaches (see Table 3.2). Their responses provide a guide to the threats of access and control, which will be expanded on later in their qualitative responses. They also indicate how the field of sports journalism has changed, and how the gatekeeping role – on both sides – is operating in the contemporary sports media environment. These responses complement aspects related to commercial factors outlined in Chapter 3. As previously mentioned, to examine these issues, the respondents were first asked to outline how important certain factors were in their work. According to the sports reporters, "Satisfying athletes" (m = 2.57) and "Satisfying team media managers or PR staff" (m = 2.03) were low priorities. When compared with the other topics in this section in the previous chapter, the mean response to satisfying team media managers or PR staff was the lowest, and satisfying athletes was slightly higher than "Conveying a positive image of the sports industry" (m = 2.53) or "Satisfying your publication's advertisers" (m = 2.44). These overall responses reflect traditional reporting aims, and indicate a dismissiveness of the reactions of content from both key potential contacts, such as athletes, and potential facilitators of interviews, such as media managers. They also indicate aspects of the "them and us" relationship between players and sports journalists (see Berry 2020), in that there is such a distance between the camps that the responses from athletes to a story do not matter.

The reaction to an article can determine whether a player talks with the journalist again, especially in a one-on-one situation, or answers their questions freely or dismissively in future media conferences. These responses were delivered against a backdrop of widespread difficulty in gaining access to newsworthy sources for interviews. They may also indicate the feeling of journalists towards media managers themselves – almost 70% said satisfying them was unimportant or a little important – and their role in deflecting or blocking access to sources. Importantly, the responses do not suggest there is a reliance on sports journalists to be friendly and supportive in their coverage based on the reactions of athletes or PR operatives. While these findings do not compare directly to previous research around cheer-leading and sports reporting in general (see Anderson 2001; Billings et al. 2011; Boyle et al. 2012; English 2017; Garrison & Salwen 1989; Hardin

2005; McEnnis 2016; Rowe 2004), they reflect a different perception to the role of being critical in reporting, or promoters of sport. These aspects have been outlined in previous chapters and prior scholarship (see Boyle 2017; English 2016a).

To examine some of the perceptions of sources linked with sports organisations in more detail, two questions related directly to sports organisations were asked (see Table 3.3). The journalists said "PR people trying to influence your stories" occurred extremely often or often 29.2% of the time, compared with 31.7% saying it occurred never or rarely (m = 2.94). In contrast, when asked how often athletes tried to influence stories (m = 1.78), the journalists said this never or rarely occurred 86.7% of the time. These responses highlight the different attitudes, in terms of attempted influence, between athletes and PR operatives. In this question, media managers or advisors could be from sports organisations or commercial entities. The results indicate there is a substantial influence from these types of staff, which highlights the attempted pressure being exerted by these bodies. Despite the attempts of PR staff to influence content, the importance of satisfying them was not high on the agenda of the sports journalists. Instead, in line with traditional newsroom approaches, there was the perception of much greater importance being placed on satisfying the audience and monitoring and scrutinising the sports industry.

Sports journalists' perceptions on sports organisations

The quantitative aspects summarise the sports journalists' views about the influence of sports organisations on their work. As explained in Chapter 3, the respondents were also asked to outline up to three key threats in the industry. The most common theme was sports organisations, particularly in relation to access and control. The responses differ from the quantitative elements in that they outline in detail what the sports journalists think about the threats, and how they are impacting on their jobs, including their roles and the content they produce, and the broader sports journalism industry. There are many concerns. The changes highlight reduced capital in the sports field for the journalists and their organisations, and indicate strong pressures and forces that impact on their ability to do their work.

A lack of access to sources, due to club regulations or decisions, was a consistent complaint. This could include rejections of requests, shutting down of key lines of questioning, or sports organisations preferring to focus on their own internal publications, such as websites or social media channels, instead of allowing interactions with media organisations (see also Sherwood et al. 2017a, 2017b). A senior television journalist said a major threat was "the internalisation of clubs in not making themselves available and disseminating their own information". This has the effect of preventing journalists from finding unique or interesting news, having to rely on the club's carefully prepared message, and leading to uniformity of content across media organisations (see Bourdieu 1998; English 2014a). The growing control of the sporting bodies reflects the changing nature of the sports field. The responses about the threats in relation to access were constant across sports, from major ones including AFL, cricket and rugby league, to those with less profile in Australia, such as tennis, motorsport, swimming and cycling.

A print reporter with more than 15 years of experience stated there had been a downward trend in interview access over the past decade, which had declined with clubs and teams not only creating their own content, but also generating their own exclusive material. "There is limited access, but a hunger for stories." Others said contemporary access was "terrible" or "impossible". One agency reporter who predominantly covers domestic sport argues "access is far worse, makes the job harder, and drives sensationalism". The gatekeeping decisions made by some journalists, in response to the changing conditions of the field over access and pressures, have led to some reporters and editors making content more exciting than it is to be different and to attract – or sustain – the audience. This type of reporting contributes to what a respondent said was "a lack of trust between journalist and player", which creates greater division and fewer interactions.

Many sports journalists outlined the need to speak to athletes to ensure fresh stories with different angles, but often were left to "pick up" quotes from other media or sports organisation sites. "We were quoting off [sports radio station] SEN a lot of the day because we didn't have access to players," one said. The quality of information when athletes interacted with journalists was also viewed as a threat. A print journalist from a major tabloid publication said media training had resulted in "dumbing down of personalities". He mentioned the public's response to the Australian cricket team's sandpaper scandal, arguing people were "so hard [on the players] because nobody could identify with anyone in the team". This highlights the broader aspects of access – and not just elements which make a journalist's job harder. It indicates that a lack of content can result in audiences not knowing the players, creating divisions between spectators and performers. Also, there is less contact and understanding in a game so valued in Australian sporting society, suggesting more macro changes in the sports field. Lack of trust of media by athletes, who can be reluctant to engage with reporters, was also cited by multiple respondents as a threat to the future of reporting.

Media managers and advisers were considered a threat to the roles of the sports journalists, and the broader industry. The responses link with the quantitative results of the journalists, who considered satisfying media managers or PR staff as unimportant in their work. A radio journalist outlined how they "restrict our ability to ask our own questions" and "everything is so managed these days". A senior broadcaster said he saw his role as being "to hold those who are spinologists to account". Not only does this highlight the changed role of former journalists now in media management or communications roles – including well-credentialled or award-winning ex-reporters – but also the control of sports organisations in shutting down questions that do not fit with their carefully managed messages. When unable to gain information from the key source, the journalist suddenly has limited options to chase the story further. In denying the question, interrupting the answer or declining an interview, the media officer is attempting to shut down the story – often successfully. A sports writer noted how club personnel could also use "confidentiality" as a way "to avoid media scrutiny". These tactics limit the information available to the public and indicate the control exercised by sports organisations. In response, a television reporter said it was an important role of sports journalists to find the stories "media departments don't want you to know about" – or the ones they are keeping hidden from the public view. Further reflecting a traditional reporting approach, a radio broadcaster said "journalists should be allowed to do work without fear or favour", instead of being coerced into "toeing the [sport organisation's] line". Respondents said this type of influence could occur through the broader sports organisation, coaches or officials, and media managers.

Clubs and teams can hold daily media conferences during the season, which allow them to argue they are being open to media, especially when demand for interviews has increased (see Baum 2020). This approach means all media outlets have the same information, with journalists moving like a swarm of bees from one opportunity to another. Generic news is not the aim of news organisations, which have traditionally sought unique content (see Bourdieu 1998; English 2014a). As one senior online journalist noted, when sports are "feeding one player a day, it turns into the best essay competition". A rugby league reporter said "it used to be you could interview players in the shower, now you can't get anywhere near them" (see also Coward 2015). He did acknowledge there were some improvements in that sport in 2019. Another remembered how in the past journalists would just "ring players, now they go through media managers". The consequences of not following the media-management protocol were outlined, with a television presenter saying there was "the risk of alienating the club if you try to go around them". A public example was highlighted by *The Sydney Morning Herald*'s chief rugby reporter, Georgina Robinson (2020), in a story about contacting Wallabies players, including prop Sekope Kepu, during the aftermath of Israel Folau's divisive comments about homosexuals. As she wrote: "*The Herald* contacted Kepu privately on April 17 but received no response, except from a Rugby Australia spokesman who expressed his displeasure that contact had been made." When journalists are being discouraged from even making contact with a source it reflects how much the field has changed.

In outlining the power of major sports organisations, an online journalist said an issue was these bodies "threatening sports writers to become their PR agents or there is no access or they are treated like crap". These types of consequences affect a journalist's access even further, reducing the journalistic and economic capital of the individual and their news organisation if they cannot speak with these figures – or accept the demands from the media managers. An agency reporter noted media managers can "make the job easier" or "very, very hard" over decisions of access not only to athletes, but also to team officials and administrators. These examples highlight the pressures and control being exerted by sports organisations in the contemporary field, which are considerably different to previous eras (see Berry 2020; Baum 2020; Blake 2012; Suggs 2016). The conditions create an environment that encourages cheerleading and support of the home side, and may influence individual and organisational gatekeeping approaches within newsrooms, which affect the quality of information being provided to audiences.

Sports organisation content and control

The broader control of sports organisations and their messages was also outlined regularly as a threat to Australian sports journalism. Reasons for this included the organisations providing their own content, setting up their own digital "news" products, and favouring their own corporate journalists over mainstream media. In effect, journalists are competing with the sports organisations while asking for their help to access their employees. This creates conflict and pressures, and highlights new forces in the sports field. An agency journalist with more than two decades of experience stated the threat was more than sporting bodies having their own website: "Organisations providing their own content, and some stories have their own bias, which limits the opportunity for critical analysis." The problem is that when journalists provide that analysis, sports organisations lose control of their message.

The larger sporting bodies have employed many communications experts who are charged with ensuring – or regaining – control, including through their own media arms. Respondents, who were speaking before the impacts of Covid-19, described the in-house websites and social media channels as "state-owned media", governing bodies "controlling their own news – not neutral or unbiased" – "mouthpieces", "a pervasive influence" and "sports and clubs thinking their club sites are more important than the media". An award-winning print columnist said a threat was "the rise of so-called media outlets that have the backing of organisations we are supposed to cover". This response again confirms the conflict over the different players and aims of those battling for position in the sports field. One senior television reporter, who covers various sports, said in-house reporting was a major threat, with "the brands taking over for themselves, with AFL House giving the best stories to themselves". Crucially, at the time of the interviews, some of these organisations with dedicated content, such as cricket.com. au, afl.com.au and nrl.com.au, had larger staff numbers than the individual media outlets reporting on them. As a print journalist who has worked for more than 30 years stated: "The Cricket Australia media arm is bigger than any other cricket media team in the country." With better resources, and the ability to prioritise their own organisation with exclusive content, it creates a major threat to mainstream sports journalism in Australia. It will be crucial to monitor the development following significant cutbacks and stand-downs in this sector created by Covid-19 (see Gleeson & Niall 2020; Harris 2020; Keoghan et al. 2020; Lalor 2020a).

An issue that combines the threats of sports organisations and commercial factors is athletes telling journalists they expect to be paid for interviews instead of doing them for free. A commercial television reporter outlined how it was "increasingly difficult to get interviews without paying". In a column, *The Australian*'s chief cricket writer Peter Lalor (2018) wrote about how sports journalism was "edging closer to an era where access is allowed only to those with a chequebook". Very few media outlets provide fees for interviews, including due to ethical constraints (see MEAA 2020). In the current financial climate, there is little spare money for media to spend, as highlighted by the reduced staff numbers and increased workloads in sports journalism. In this space, the rise of first-person sites for players (see *AthletesVoice* 2020) was also seen by multiple respondents as a threat to sports journalism. Knowing that this type of "coverage" is available – and with the mistrust between players and the media mentioned earlier (see Berry 2020; Jackson 2019) – athletes can be reluctant to deal openly with mainstream media. These relatively new elements in sports media and journalism are having a major influence in changing the field, and short-changing sports journalists.

New rules of the game

Sports journalism in Australia is being heavily influenced by sports organisations, who control the thing reporters crave the most – information. With the strengthened financial position of sports organisations over the past decade, in contrast to the declining bottom line in many news organisations, it is evident that sports journalism is being more isolated in the field by these external forces and pressures. The rules of the game played between sports journalism and sports organisations have changed. It is no longer a symbiotic relationship (see McChesney 1989; Mirer 2019; Sherwood et al. 2017a), but one where sports journalism is more dominated than dominant. This substantial altering of sports journalism's place in the field means it experiences less influence, produces more uniform content, and its journalists have access to the same limited sources. In this environment, sports journalism faces significant threats to the future of the industry through restrictions to access and the control exerted by sports organisations.

The sports journalists in this study clearly view the controls being placed on them as a major threat to their work, their publications, their industry and also at times the broader sporting society. In relation to the two major threats outlined in this book, the restrictions over access appear a greater concern to them than commercial factors, because they impact on their day-to-day roles and routines, and affect their ability to perform their jobs to high standards. What the sports journalists say about their perceptions to access, media managers and athletes reflects a traditional independent approach to their reporting and gatekeeping of content. Again, it is important to note there may be differences between the journalists' perceptions and their actions (see Tandoc et al. 2013), with content not being examined in this study. However, the changes created by the rise of sports organisations have had major alterations to macro and micro elements within the field. With less power, and a desire to retain their employment, there is potential for sometimes dubious journalistic gatekeeping and ethical decisions to ensure the sports organisations and athletes remain on side. There are also the pressures of having to produce content each day that audiences will find interesting enough to select their organisation instead of the glut of other news media and sports organisation publications available.

5 Suggestions for the future of sports journalism

At this critical point in sport journalism's history, it is essential to outline suggestions for reframing the area as a more independent sector. The way forward can involve idealistic and more realistic changes to face the range of threats. Sports journalism in Australia is experiencing many difficulties, as outlined in the previous chapters, and is being dominated and controlled by sports organisations and commercial entities. It is clear that the current approaches to combating these threats are not working. Financial influences are a major element in these decisions, but the current crisis is broader and affects not just the bottom line, but also content, roles, routines, ethics, journalists, newsrooms and audiences. Challenges including the changing media environment, control by sports organisations, lack of access to key figures, and the infiltration of commercial aspects in sports coverage have led to sports journalism experiencing substantial reductions in both economic and journalistic capital. By attempting to do as much as possible to satisfy the market, many newsrooms have made their situation worse. With shrinking staff and financial figures, declining newsroom conditions and subservience to external organisations, the environment is primed for a change of direction to assist in regaining capital and control. While the suggestions can be easily dismissed and not considered achievable, the question needs to be asked: How bad can things get for sports journalism in Australia? There are fewer journalists in mainstream publications, closing media outlets, stories dependent on press releases and media opportunities, sports organisations creating a virtual monopoly on exclusive and general content, the dominance of copy from agencies or sister publications, and restrictions over travel. It is time to attempt something different. This was particularly relevant as media and sports organisations wrestled with Covid-19-impacts on budgets in 2020 and influenced their short- and long-term planning.

These struggles provide an opportunity for the media to redraw boundaries and relationships. Based on the results in the survey, some suggestions for the future will be outlined, particularly in retaining independence and relevance. These comments are not written from an ivory tower, or based on smugness and sneering at an industry that is struggling and was better in the old days. It is critical to note it is the role of the sports media scholar to monitor and scrutinise what is happening in sports journalism (Wei 2019). The conclusions in this Chapter are also based on the responses of the 120 sports journalists. These suggestions are offered in an attempt to boost an important area of journalism, one that is essential in finding stories that matter to sports audiences and are not based on public relations and copy-approved drivel.

The field

The current reality is that sports organisations are dominating the sports field in Australia, and these pressures are having serious impacts on sports journalism. The main threat outlined was the access and control being exerted by sports organisations, with their teams of media advisors, in-house publications and restrictions on granting interview requests. As Figure 5.1 shows, the sports organisations are the major players in the sports field, particularly when considering the high-profile sports which dominate the market through broadcasting deals. Sports organisations also schedule the seasons and fixture lists, employ the key talent in players, coaches and administrators, and produce their own content. This provides them with power, economic capital and the ability to exert their dominance over other players in the field. These forces are relatively new, particularly in the sports media space, and have had huge implications for sports journalism.

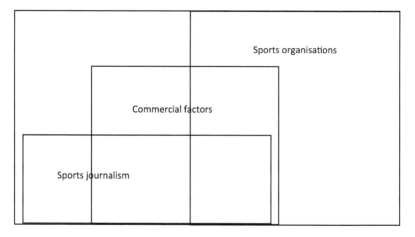

Figure 5.1 Elements of the sports field in Australia

Sports organisations cannot operate completely without other commercial partners, including those in the media with their broadcast capabilities. Commercial factors have a distinct place in the field, and concerns over their presence and impact on sports journalism have been outlined in Chapter 3. The commercial elements are both external and internal to news organisations, but are linked. One of the reasons there has been such a change in operations in sports journalism is the declining overall financial position of media since the Global Financial Crisis. With fewer resources, news organisations have made concessions to the market in an effort to retain economic capital. These decisions have often come at the expense of journalistic capital. Media organisations are corporate entities, and are profit driven apart from the government-funded ABC and SBS, which can result in a greater entertainment focus than public-interest approach. But the aims of journalism companies are built on foundations of truth, accuracy and independence (see Mindich 1998; Schudson 2001; Tuchman 1972).

Based on the factors outlined in this book, sports journalism is suffering as a dominated entity in the sports field, with reduced levels of capital. These factors are why sports journalism's place is smaller and overshadowed by the commercial factors and sports organisations. While sports journalism has always had strong entertainment aspects and close links with sporting bodies, there has traditionally been independence in the workings of media outlets (see Boyle 2006; Boyle & Haynes 2009; Rowe 2007; Zion et al. 2011). In Figure 5.1 it is evident that the overall approach being taken by sports newsrooms is not working, both in how they are currently operating, and how they are responding to threats in the field. If there is no change in the way these departments function, the future will be effectively providing public relations material for sports and commercial organisations, instead of reporting that is independent, critical and complimentary at times, and uncovers the true workings of sporting bodies, clubs and athletes. There is the potential for sports journalists to become what they have traditionally despised – mouthpieces for sports organisations and commercial entities.

The ideal solution?

There is a prevailing feeling that everything was better in the old days, so going back is the only way forward. Newsrooms were better in the 20th century, when budgets were bigger, travel and expenses were generous, staff were on hand to run copy or errands, advertising in legacy publications was the only way to promote a product, circulations and viewer numbers were huge, it was possible to hang out at the bar with athletes, and there was no filing for websites. A time when sports organisations did not have media departments, were often run by volunteers who did not always seem to know what they were doing, and when receiving a press release by fax was an achievement. When newspapers, radio and television were the only ways to get a story to mass audiences, and sports journalists held the power to keep information in – or out. Back then sports journalists were a dominant force in the field, and were able to demand access to key sources as soon as they could reach the nearest landline, and the comments would be in the paper the next morning or on television later that night. A return to these conditions is fortunately not achievable, because there were elements of past reporting that needed improving. A journalist's role is to watch and scrutinise power – not to have most of it – so the attitudes of the past were not perfect.

Sports journalism has enjoyed golden periods but the industry has had its problems traditionally, especially around the ethics of cheerleading and bias (see Anderson 2001; Billings et al. 2011; Boyle et al. 2012; Garrison & Salwen 1989; Hardin 2005; Marchetti 2005; McEnnis 2016; Rowe 2004). A rule of reporting is always avoid being seen as part of the team – and avoid players thinking journalists are part of the team. Life in the past was often too cosy between the parties, particularly around late-night, off-the-record bar sessions. However, there would be definite benefits to sports journalists staying in the same hotels as the players at times to allow more healthy relationships to develop – if only newsrooms could afford it. Both media and sports have transformed over the past three decades and the misty-eyed romance of days past could not be replicated. Even if they were better. That does not mean things cannot change, and elements of the past reinforced in contemporary reporting. A return to some more traditional approaches would be beneficial, both to journalists and audiences.

The reality

The contemporary reality is sports organisations and commercial factors are dominating sports journalism. Sports journalism has become a smaller player with less capital in the sports field, and its existence is being threatened by the commercial influences and impact of sports organisations with expanding power and control. It is possible to feel sorry for the journalists and organisations who have been involved in watching the shift from newsrooms being the dominant players to having to beg for exclusives or "information subsidies" (see Sherwood et al. 2017b). But these journalistic players have not always been innocent bystanders. As Sherwood et al. (2017b, p. 1005) have noted, sports journalism in Australia "has been complicit in ceding control of the sport media agenda to professional sport organisations". This power will be difficult to get back, but steps can be taken to regain more control – at least in what newsrooms themselves are producing. News organisations would benefit from seeing the sports organisations as the opposition, and being focused on beating them to stories – even if they are starting behind because of access to sources. Essentially, the content provided by sports organisations is an attempt to put sports journalism out of business – or at least applying pressure so it occupies a smaller place on the sideline. This may alter as sport resumes after Covid-19 and there have been small signs of sports organisations being more open, with the AFL offering all players by phone after matches when the competition resumed in 2020. Whether the sports organisations decide to relax the strong positions they have developed over the past decade and return to a method of cooperation to spread the word of their games and athletes in the longer term is another matter. Giving up power is never easy, especially if officials are not convinced of the benefits. The situation in many cases outlined by survey respondents is that the current levels of control by sports organisations and commercial operations make it extremely challenging for sports journalists to fulfil their roles properly, especially in comparison with previous eras. For journalists to be able to improve their status in the field, it is time to change the way they do their jobs. Considering the current state of sports journalism in Australia – and other nations – there is a need for some risk taking to regain a greater presence in the field.

New (and old) roles and routines

The initial steps involve journalists and newsrooms striving for more independence from commercial and sports organisations, including less reliance on being fed content by sports organisations and media managers. New roles and routines, as well as dusting off some of the approaches that have been crucial to traditional reporting, must be developed. These alterations include changes to content to make it less uniform, a greater range of sources, fostering more fruitful relationships between players and media, and training. Following widespread industry transformations, it is important to recognise life in a sports newsroom is more difficult for journalists than in previous decades. As stated throughout the book, the losses of economic capital have caused significant cost-cutting, fewer staff and greater workloads. This is unlikely to ease, especially due to the ramifications of Covid-19 on the news and sports industries. For there to be a shift in the way sport is reported, changes are required at the routines gatekeeping level. However, individual journalists cannot make these switches on their own. A shift in attitude at the organisational level is also essential.

Shifts in content

The culture of newsrooms is embedded with the importance of stories from major sports, and now relies heavily on media opportunities, press releases and information subsidies as part of news-day routines (see Hutchins & Boyle 2017; Sherwood et al. 2017b). Not missing a major story is a key role of sports journalists, especially in high-capital or "core" sports, such as AFL, rugby league, rugby union and cricket (see Bourdieu 1998; English 2014b; Schultz-Jorgensen 2005). However, with so much information available on other platforms, including those of sports organisations, and the speed of publication on online and social media, major stories are being missed by newsrooms every day. Stories broken by competing outlets are simply re-written or re-packaged for websites. What news organisations have historically worried about missing does not always contribute much journalistic value in a digital world.

This environment provides editors and journalists with an opportunity to alter their approaches to some areas of content to avoid the current uniformity. Despite the shifts over the past three decades, the way sports journalism is presented across media has remained relatively stable. Television and radio sports bulletins are before the weather, using the same formats of packages or live crosses. In newspapers, the biggest story or match report on the most important game is the back-page lead. Quotes from sources dominate stories, and news articles without them are rare. In the hierarchy of comments, a quote from a player usually beats everything, even if it is bland and from a media conference. International sports are often run as briefs, columnists get a thumbnail image, feature stories appear intermittently and are generally saved for the weekend, and ghosted columns from athletes will be heavily promoted but contain little insight. Mistakes will occur in headlines, introductions and captions, due to the lack of sub-editing and higher workloads. Coverage is male dominated, and photographs of female athletes are more likely to be in passive than active poses (see English et al. 2019; Horky & Nieland 2013; Schultz-Jorgensen 2005; Sherry et al. 2016; Sherwood et al. 2017c). These attitudes to female sport have also been seen across media platforms. "Minor" sports are included deep into the section, often where the women's coverage is hidden, and near the small-font results and league tables – despite them being available so easily online, or via social media.

Instead, sports coverage is focused on a small range of "core sports" (English 2014b; see also Schultz-Jorgensen 2005). Even in the middle of summer, when cricket is the main focus, an AFL item can lead the sports coverage in the *Herald Sun* in Melbourne or a rugby league story in *The Courier-Mail* in Brisbane. Why? In part because it has always been the way, and that these roles, routines and gatekeeping decisions are ingrained in sports journalism's culture. Rugby union, soccer and horse racing gain regular coverage too, but there is limited reporting of other sports (see English 2014b; English et al. 2019). Including different sports in prominent positions can help to alter the "core sports" landscape. Adopting this approach regularly would require overlooking contemporary and historical attitudes to reporting. As well as the "we've always done it this way" view, the current obsession with analytics in so many newsrooms provides obstacles to delivering varied coverage. Many departments have monitors where analytics are visible from reporters' desks, and metrics become a focus on gatekeeping decisions. Stories and sports that receive more clicks are prioritised while smaller sports are left well behind. The approaches to analytics were evident in the survey in a question focusing on how often respondents experienced "a reliance on metrics and audience data" (see Table 3.3). Thirty-five percent said this occurred extremely often or often, compared with 34.2% who said it occurred never or rarely (m = 3.03). Unsurprisingly, online journalists perceived the highest reliance on metrics (m = 4.09), followed by magazine journalists (m = 3.33), who have also experienced a heavy shift towards an online focus, and television (m = 3.12), which has traditionally been ratings driven. Print journalists were below the mean (m = 2.89), but ahead of radio (m = 2.72). Agency journalists (m = 2.17) were the lowest, unsurprisingly, due to their role of writing for subscribing organisations rather than audiences directly.

To produce content that focuses on a wider variety of topics, journalists and editors need to make more gatekeeping decisions in conjunction with analytics, rather than relying solely on them. Asking editors and journalists to pay less attention to key sports can be easily dismissed as ridiculous, especially in an era when financial conditions are sluggish at best, particularly after the impact of Covid-19. More hits equal more – or at least some – revenue. This suggestion to move coverage away from the breadwinning sports is likely to be anathema to sports editors and news directors. However, it is an aspect to consider in widening the scope of coverage, moving back from the major sports organisations that are dominating sports newsrooms with restrictions and controls, and providing reporting more reflective of the diversity of sport. Each media company's commercial considerations are critical to this decision, but news publications can appear increasingly old-fashioned and risk-averse in contemporary media.

Adopting content changes is a way to attempt to appeal to a broader market, while not having to rely on suffocating media management for access to key sources. An example occurs with Super Netball, which English et al. (2019) found received between 0.99% and 3.26% of total stories in the sports sections of eight metropolitan or national newspapers. This was during the 2017 season, when interest in netball was at its highest that year. As previously stated, coverage is traditionally dominated by male sport (see Sherwood et al. 2017c), but a more professional approach to women's sport has occurred in Australia in the past five years. While different types of stories are noticeable, including around the start and conclusion of women's events, there has been a slow uptake in sections of the media. Yet these are the areas which may provide journalistic and economic benefits to sports newsrooms in the longer term. In the United Kingdom, *The Daily Telegraph* started "*Telegraph* Women's Sport" in 2019. It combines a monthly print supplement with a dedicated website, weekly newsletter and social media content. Produced under the direction of a women's sport editor, it has the aim of "making a commitment to transform the profile of women's sport and its visibility in the media" (*Telegraph* Women's Sport 2019). Resources are clearly an issue in Australian media, but this is an example of what sustained coverage of female sport can look like. Similar approaches can be applied to other sports, regardless of gender. Given the state of sports journalism in Australia, a longer-term vision is required if it is going to regain capital and ensure a sustainable place in the sports field. Building a publication with a variety of sports that provides greater diversity and attracts both the general and specialist sports reader takes time. This is something newsrooms can consider in an attempt to avoid the current approaches to uniformity, and to build journalistic and economic capital to strengthen their place in the field.

The search for new sources

To enhance this shift towards different and diverse content, pursuing a greater variety of sources is crucial, particularly when many players and coaches are being prevented from speaking outside of carefully orchestrated media events by public relations staff. Rowe (2007) is among those who have noted the small pool of sources used by sports journalists, while Steen (2015, p. 14) has outlined the importance of a full and "regularly replenished contacts book". These figures need to be more than just club media managers (see Sherwood et al. 2017b) who can be useful in gaining basic details, but a limiting factor when journalists are attempting to uncover unique, newsworthy information (see also Hutchins & Boyle 2017). As one respondent in the survey stated, it is the role of sports journalists to find the stories "media departments don't want you to know about". The industry as a whole, including those journalists working on desk shifts re-writing content, needs to re-adopt this approach to eliminate the reliance on sports organisations providing the information – and the access.

In contrast, chasing different sources and gaining varied angles on news topics would help newsrooms return to setting the agenda on a greater range of issues, which other media organisations would then follow up (see Bourdieu 1998). This would create more unique and interesting items, rather than the same fare provided by the packs of reporters drifting across media conferences, either in person or online. Phoning sources has traditionally been a major role and routine of sports journalism, but with the dominance of sports organisations' media managers, and the steady stream of content being delivered to inboxes, there appears to be less reliance on this vital news-gathering method. A greater insistence on calls for fresh comments, at the routines and organisational levels, would expand the options for sources, increase diversity of coverage and change patterns of parts of the reporting process. Every sport has hundreds of former players, coaches and administrators who can provide information and opinions on current news and events. This has been a staple of past sports media coverage, and is still practised by some reporters, including those in the study. It is a tactic that appears to be in decline due to the control being exerted by sports organisations, and the workloads of journalists. Audiences want to hear from those closest to the action, such as star players and coaches making the crucial decisions. But when comments are sanitised and bland in most of those media opportunities or interactions that even the most teasing clickbait headline cannot make them appealing, there is little point running them. Drawing on a greater variety of sources can increase the overall quality of information, create better storytelling, and offer more context to audiences.

Searching for more voices is especially important for those sports journalists who spend most time on the desk in editing or production shifts, and whose role is to turn media releases or news-agency copy into online content. While recognising the high demands of the job, these often-young employees need to look for other talent in stories, be sceptical, add information or verify it. Training and mentoring from senior journalists are critical, but this has been another area that has declined due to changes in budgets and workloads. For the industry to shift, these crucial practices of journalism, which have been devalued in the race for quick-and-easy online content, need to be restored. Altering these news-gathering approaches can ensure more accurate information, avoid embarrassing mistakes such as the James Faulkner (ABC 2019) "boyfriend" example from Chapter 2, and provide extra value to stories based on – or copied entirely from – media releases. Again, these alterations rely on shifts at an organisational gatekeeping level, as well as at the individual and routines levels.

If these switches to sources and news-gathering are made, the results may be that sports organisations observe the different types of content and change the quality and direction of the public contributions from their athletes. If the bland offerings of athletes and coaches are ignored by major media, it loosens the control sports organisations have over the media's message. This is a way newsrooms can attempt to regain independence and increase journalistic capital that, again, could lead to greater economic capital in the medium term. Sports organisations have a major advantage with the contacts they employ and the content they own, but there are stories in all sports that are not being told. Billings (2019) has discussed the aims of journalism, including in sport, which are to be best or be different. This simple sentence is key in newsrooms positioning themselves for the future. As the snapshot of *The Australian*'s coverage in Chapter 2 highlights, much of the content in modern sports reporting is uniform, and past research has shown there are relatively few exclusives (see Bourdieu 1998; English 2014a). Recent changes, including News Corp Australia's move to a national newswire, increases the likelihood of more similar material across the nation's publications. This creates an opportunity for organisations to produce different coverage to attract new audiences while continuing to entertain existing ones. Otherwise the question remains, why should people consume a publication when it is so similar to the competition? These changes could be slow and difficult, but are worth attempting in the medium term to attempt to keep sports journalism relevant.

The use of unnamed sources is also increasingly problematic. With the rise of media managers at clubs there has been an explosion of unattributed quotes from team spokespeople or "insiders", who are pushing the commercial or sports-organisation line. As outlined in the MEAA (2020) Code of Ethics, the aim is to attribute information to the source, which gives accountability to the details and increases the journalistic capital of the story and source. A senior print sports journalist in the study remembered, around the Alan Jones "Cash for Comment" scandal in 1999, when reporters were told "no unattributed quotes unless you could sustain the argument with the editor. It's a shame it's slipped". The journalist noted in the current environment "sports reporters have made up quotes from a club insider" due to the demands of the job. This is a one-off anecdotal comment that highlights the potential for ethical breaches in a place where shortcuts can occur due to workloads, restricted access to key sources, and the demands of writing to deadline. In this space, the request of the journalist that the policy on unattributed quotes "should be back to how it was before" is a sensible one. Not only would it diminish the role of the "nameless" spokesperson providing comments from sports organisations or PR companies that raise doubts over the quality of the information, but it would improve the quality of journalistic information for audiences.

The state of the industry

In reflecting on the current state and future prospects of the industry, respondents outlined many problems with the sector, and made suggestions for boosting sports journalism. Clearly, from these comments, it is hard to imagine the industry getting worse in terms of access and control. The journalists also discussed more macro issues surrounding the general state of the industry. As English (2019) noted, there was a gloomy overall perception, with less than a third very satisfied or extremely satisfied about the current state of sports journalism (m = 2.95), or the future of sports journalism (m = 2.85). The latter result had decreased in comparison with Nicholson et al. (2011). It is easy to see why this is the case considering the threats and recent changes to the broader industry, and sport specifically. Some of these aspects have intensified during the Covid-19 pandemic. In this new environment, journalists, newsrooms and organisations need to resolve to fight back instead of accepting their lowly and declining place in the field.

Interestingly, some of the comments suggesting ways to improve the state of sports journalism came from senior newsroom figures, the type of people who have been able to make or lobby for these changes. It highlights how many of the gatekeeping decisions and roles and routines of sports journalism have become entrenched. One print journalist, who held a senior editing position, outlined how on a game day the lead story in the sports section has always been the match report. He argued this was outdated, because anyone interested in the contest would already know the score and key moments from a range of online and offline sources before the newspaper was available. In the introduction of these articles, match writers attempt to "push the story forward", rather than looking back, and focus on the game's turning point to offer something new to readers. However, they are still reporting on a contest many people already know the basic details about. The senior journalist suggested the lead story on the back page be an opinion or analysis piece from the senior sports writer or columnist. "In this age, people know what the score was from TV, radio or social media, so the match report is less important." The sports journalist, who has written across multiple sports, said currently the stories "around the edge of the page", such as columns or quotes pieces from the dressing rooms, provided new and interesting information. News publications and journalists say they experiment with story selection – or gatekeeping approaches – along with analytics and internal research, but in this case it may be that that the main story on a match day is being ignored for the information journalists think they are supposed to supply. Altering the back-page-lead process would require a committed shift in sports journalism's culture and gatekeeping attitudes, but is the type of experiment that could engage more readers.

The search to provide something different to inform and broaden audiences is not limited to print and online. Broadcast journalists also attempt to tell viewers and listeners something different. A common role and routine of sports journalists was summed up by a veteran radio journalist, who said content needed to be "unique" in order to attract people. "Everyone does the same thing, so journalists need to work harder at finding different or unique stories." The answers to solving problems around content are not easy ones, especially when the sports journalists themselves are already working hard and across multiple platforms. In the survey, 60% of respondents were publishing stories across two platforms, and a third were operating across three or more (English 2019). Sports journalism is no longer a job for long pub lunches and lazy days watching the game, but that does not mean it can be allowed as an industry to ignore vital elements needed for reform. Finding content that is new, interesting and different from that being supplied by sports organisations is essential to ensure sports journalism is healthy in the future. This would have advantages for increasing journalistic capital, and diversity of information may also lead to increases in economic capital as broader audiences become aware of – and interested in – the revamped content strategy.

Protecting content from commercial interests

While many aspects of sports journalism need to move forward, a return to more pure forms of information delivery would be welcome as a way to increase journalistic capital and deflect many of the commercial influences forced on newsrooms. Commercial factors have been an expanding presence in story content (see English 2013, 2016c), both in allowing what broadcasters and commentators can say, and in what is being included in text-based stories. The corporate creep of commercial mentions has been an increasing feature since the Global Financial Crisis, with newsrooms submitting to the demands of sponsors, advertisers or player managers, in return for access to subjects (see Baum 2020; Hooper 2014). In some cases, the inclusion may be subtle, such as photographing an athlete in a sponsor's shirt, but in others the commercial deal is so obvious the story should be accommodated by an "advertorial" banner. The difficulty in the choice of whether journalists should accept or dismiss these types of requests is understood, but too much power and influence has been given to the commercial entities so they now think they can expect this type of advertising intrusion to be readily accommodated.

The demands outlined by Baum (2020) for an interview can be extensive. That Baum wrote about the experience is also newsworthy and an indication that media organisations will not always be pushed around by commercial pressures. More coverage telling the truth about corporate operations and their tactics could dissuade them from making such heavy-handed "invitations". Journalistic capital and ethics still matter, but it may be that only senior figures such as Baum, an associate editor who has been a sports journalist for more than three decades, are in a position to decline these requests. The same may not be available to younger or more inexperienced reporters, who could feel obliged – or, worse, see it as the way of this new world – to accept these demands. It is also relevant to note the ethical breaches in relation to gifts, benefits, direct or indirect payment, and advertising or commercial considerations that undermine accuracy or independence and influence stories (MEAA 2020). In accepting an interview and then writing about the athlete's association with a corporate organisation, the independence of the journalist and organisation is compromised because they are effectively being told what to include.

These commercial mentions may be seen as the new rules of the game, and that it is better to include them than see a journalist lose their job because of worsening financial considerations, or they may get another interview in the future, or the organisation could pick up an advertisement or some other commercial benefit. But these decisions are unethical, and affect the journalistic capital of the organisation. Similar to Sherwood et al.'s (2017) conclusion that sports journalists have ceded control to media managers in sports organisations, they have also given up some of their ethical, moral and journalistic obligations in allowing corporations to infiltrate the sports pages and airwaves so regularly. "Buy an ad" used to be the response to these types of queries, rather than "What do we have to mention to get the interview?" It is another example of newsrooms yielding to commercial pressures in the hope they can retain a place in the field (see Bourdieu 1998). As outlined in Figure 5.1, that place is now smaller and being dominated by external factors. If nothing changes in the approaches taken by organisations and journalists, there will be even less space for sports journalism. Throughout the results and analysis in this book, it is clear sports journalism is experiencing some of the "deeply problematic consequences" outlined by Schultz-Jorgensen (2005), after allowing the sports industry to set the agenda for sports coverage (see also Horky & Nieland 2013; Rowe 2007). This development has become more concerning over the past decade, at least in Australia.

While much of this analysis has focused on text-based articles, there are also recommendations for broadcasters. Commercial complications can be more complex due to rights and regulations, including how commentators respond to governing bodies. As mentioned in Chapter 1, the situation during the Cricket World Cup in 2019 was so bad Michael Holding reportedly said commentators were being controlled "to the point of censorship". A combination of broadcast rights deals, conflicts of interest across media markets, such as News Corp Australia with cricket coverage, and the anodyne comments of many former athletes – including those who have conflicts of interest themselves – contributes to making this area of sports journalism bland. Imagine the situation if sports broadcasters and their "expert" contributors were able to speak freely and to praise and be critical when necessary? The employment of more journalists in these roles instead of ex-players would certainly help rectify this situation, as well as allowing broadcasters autonomy to offer their opinions. For this to happen, changes at media level and organisational gatekeeping levels are required (see Shoemaker & Vos 2009).

Sports broadcasting is an area of sports journalism in which collective shifts, involving a variety of media organisations, would be beneficial. This would appear less likely in a broadcast market where huge sums of money rule decisions over content, ethics and judgement. Journalists in the survey noted how the cross-ownership in News Corp Australia had "compromised" coverage. Unfortunately, when media organisations themselves are blurring the lines between commercial and editorial content, it makes it increasingly difficult for widespread change. In the meantime, sports organisations and commercial companies can increase their economic capital while the media organisations lose both journalistic and economic capital, according to the balance sheets (see, for example, Kruger 2019). One way out of this commercial trap for sports journalism is to report and present independently, and operate with fewer concerns over the grip of sports and commercial organisations. It also means sports newsrooms can operate less like an advertising agency (Schultz-Jorgensen 2005) and more like a traditional news operation. There are major concerns in this area of sports journalism and it is essential to note again that the environment has changed, with more pervasive commercial factors and internal financial restrictions among most media organisations. The times are not easy for journalists and their departments. But there is a pressing need to regain control over publishing information and for it to be "pure" and more traditional in a journalistic sense, rather than stained by commercial influence.

"Them versus us"

The relationship between the media and athletes has often been one of dispute, particularly in the contemporary era (see Berry 2020). Distance between the two parties has made the dynamic worse for sports journalists and – while they may not see it – the players who now have little understanding of the media's role (see Wingard 2020). The inclusion of more layers of management in the years before the Covid-19 crisis, through media staff at sports organisations and personal agents, has added further barriers to what were often smoother relations – and involved easier access – between journalists and athletes (see Blake 2012; Jackson 2019). It needs to be noted that some athletes and coaches are happy being shielded from journalists, operating in safe, media-managed spaces. This can be due to having a general dislike of not being able to control the information they deliver (see Wingard 2020), bad experiences with media in which information was not presented as they believed they had said it, worrying about saying something to upset their team or organisation, or not wanting to be part of the public discussion space. As in other areas of media, there are also different perceptions of what each side sees as "truth", or the interpretation of facts or comments following an interview. At times, the relationship can be antagonistic, due to journalists wanting to report on a sensitive story, or suggesting an out-of-form player be dropped. But the current approach by athletes and sports organisations to media has led to less honest, less entertaining, less truthful and less "pure" journalistic information being conveyed to supporters and audiences.

Respondents indicated a lack of trust was an element keeping players and media apart, which in turn affected access and interview quality. It seems sports journalism in Australia has been unable to strike the balance between the cosy past, and the too-distant present. Writing about sources who may also be friends you drink with on tour can create ethical dilemmas based on honesty, trust, independence, compromise, complicity, bias and cheerleading (see Boyle & Haynes 2009; Horky & Nieland 2013; Schultz-Jorgensen 2005; Rowe 2007). It can be argued easily that journalists of previous eras were often too close to their sources, and that regular off-the-record pub briefings resulted in ignoring information that might have been either entertaining or in the public interest (see Berry 2020; Blake 2012). That method also had merits, in that grievances could be discussed and understanding gained – even if not agreement. It was an important place for learning background and context, which could help journalists be more informed about events, and writing more "truth". It was also a way to ensure one-on-one interactions that were not facilitated – or attended – by a media manager. At the other end of the pole is the current "them versus us" (Berry 2020) opposition, which occurs both in Australia and internationally.

It is important to recognise the debate over who counts as an "expert". Ex-players in the commentary box are given credit for their on-field knowledge, but can easily dismiss the contributions of journalists who they say do not understand the game because they never played it. There is resentment, too, from the journalists who view ex-professionals as "hi-jacking" their jobs. Former professionals often follow the public-relations-style demands of bland commentary and cheerleading (see Harman 2019; Knox 2020; Lemon 2015). Journalists, in contrast, are more likely to offer different sides to an issue, or at least ask more probing questions. If the quality of information being provided is accurate or well argued, then it should not matter how much of an "expert" the journalist is.

Currently, the "them versus us" approach means neither "side" gains an understanding of what the other is trying to achieve, and are kept at a distance. Instead, media managers or personal managers take on the role as informant or information blocker. This situation is still creating problems for modern journalists, except now the aim is to gain any information, rather than the dilemma of previous generations who were more often deciding what had to be left out. In the current environment, being close to a player can mean effectively being a spokesperson for them to avoid upsetting them. Alternatively, for the rest there is the option of being free to write more critically, since there is little danger of damage to athlete-sources. In theory, this leaves the journalists able to pursue unpopular but public-interest news and commentary without worrying about the fallout from the subjects – or at least those not in the media department. Respondents indicated they did not worry about satisfying athletes, or team media managers or PR staff in their stories, and athletes never or rarely tried to influence their stories. If the reactions from the players and media managers do not matter to the journalists, then it helps them be more critical when necessary. However, there seems to be an over-riding concern that journalists will be sidelined by the media managers of clubs or teams, which indicates they are holding back on their reporting at times. Ultimately, the scoreboard in this game shows the media is not influenced by the reactions of athletes, and athletes think the media write negative things about them. The players prefer to do media through their own team, individual or athlete-first sites (see *Athletes Voice* 2020; Wingard 2020), which gives them greater control over their information. It is a cycle that continues to keep players and media apart.

As a starting point, it is important for athletes to have an understanding of the role of sports journalism. It is also essential that players know journalists are not their promotional support crew – and definitely not one of the team. This is a valuable reminder for reporters themselves, who talk about not being "supporters" but do not always follow the advice. Alternatively, sports journalists must also understand they are writing and broadcasting for audiences, not attempting to gain or retain favour with a player to ensure another interview or occasional quote. The current climate certainly offers opportunities for journalists to avoid being "owned" by their sources and to be critical when necessary. As Boyle and Haynes (2009, p. 183) note, "sports journalism should be about reporting, enquiring, explaining and at times holding to account sports on behalf of fans". Boyle (2006, p. 125) argues "promoting the game is simply not what sports journalism is about", and instead what occurs on the field of play needs to be "the most important driver in shaping journalistic opinion and comment". Overall, sports reporting should be based on the journalistic foundation of presenting the truth accurately, operating with public-interest aims, while reflecting the entertainment aspects of the game. In the current reality, there are many factors and threats influencing sports journalists in their work, particularly around commercial elements and access and control exerted by sports organisations. By reporting freely as suggested earlier, there may be punishment from the external sources, such as even less access, or denied applications for accreditation. This is where having a broader field of sources for stories can be advantageous, allowing reporters to circumvent the controls placed on them by sports organisations.

Writing in the United Kingdom, where similar distance exists between players and media, rugby correspondent Robert Kitson (2020) suggested it could help the media-athlete relationship "if more players were also encouraged to see the benefits of engaging with the media, to look past the occasional wince-inducing headline and recognise the opportunity to project themselves, both as athletes and as human beings". Is this wishful thinking from a journalist who has worked for a major media organisation for more than two decades, or a way to ensure more access and interest from athletes' media interactions? One shift that has occurred in this space in Australia is a small number of journalists being sent to cover inter-state matches of the domestic Twenty20 cricket tournament, with flights and accommodation in the team hotel being paid by a state association. Respondents in the survey say this has led to greater access, including being able to have breakfast with the players at times, and has helped in building relationships. It is an example of how media management by those who have formerly been involved in reporting can help break down some of the issues over lack of access and distance. This is an encouraging change that is also disturbing, with an external commercial organisation providing the funding contributions for "independent" journalists to travel for work. While in the current financial state this type of support has become more common (see English 2016c), this example sums up the threats influencing Australian sports journalism. Even when something is happening to help, it comes with commercial and ethical strings attached.

The importance of training

A final suggestion for helping sports journalists is to provide further training. This recommendation is another that may not be popular in industry, especially for experienced journalists who know everything about the area. Greater forms of training are particularly valuable for more junior journalists, who are often filling the desk-based or production roles and have less access to senior mentors than in the past when they delivered much of the on-the-job teaching. A reduction in budgets has created this problem and shifting the focus to further role-specific education is difficult in the current climate. Again, it is a valuable point to consider in helping regain capital and gatekeeping influence in sports journalism. McEnnis (2019) has written about training Sky Sports News television journalists in England. These sessions were developed partly due to the complexity of technological change in the industry, but also because of "the growing commercialisation and globalisation of professional sports" (McEnnis 2019, p. 199). Teaching occurs in practical areas, but also in more foundational spaces around ethics, journalism's role as a Fourth Estate, sports journalists' positioning over cheerleading, holding power to account, and the political economy of the sports media.

While noting the industry's scepticism in the value of academic training, McEnnis (2019, p. 205) states the aim of the course is "to raise professional standards" within the sports newsroom and to help discard the toy department description. As Sherwood and English (2019b, p. 152) explain, this model could provide a guide for Australian newsrooms experiencing similar challenges and forces to those in England, and be effective in building bridges between "the industry-academic divide". While this type of training would be beneficial for sports journalists, particularly for those who are junior members of the profession, it would be particularly effective for the former players who enter media roles, giving them an understanding of the broader principles of journalism and broadcasting. During the course of this research, there were respondents who did not see value in academic scholarship on sports journalism. However, even having sports journalists considering the point of their work can help them understand the broader state of the industry, including the historical practices and approaches. With this knowledge, the sports journalists themselves may be able to plot a way forward for an industry that appears to have lost focus of what is both important and what is able to be attained, within the constraints of their organisations and the pressures of the field.

A road to recovery

Sports journalism is experiencing a crisis due to a range of dominant threats, leaving it a shadow of its past role. The decline in both journalistic and economic capital has caused substantial changes to the sports journalism and sport fields in Australia, as well as many other parts of the world. The suggestions made in this chapter are provided as a way to overcome some of the threats and enable sports journalism to stay in the game. In an increasingly complex field, sports journalism needs to regain its relevance and remain in a position where it can continue making important contributions to society, particularly by providing truthful, independent and verified information to audiences. Throughout this book, which is predominantly based on the survey responses of Australian sports journalists, the challenges and obstacles created by the threats have been outlined, especially in relation to the influence of commercial factors and the power and control of sports organisations. It has resulted in changes to the traditional roles and routines of reporting, and opened up sports journalism to being more reliant on external organisations. Some of the historical approaches to news-gathering have been lost, forgotten or overlooked as individuals and broader newsrooms have given up control to – and been compromised by – commercial factors and sports organisations.

Overall, sports journalists in the survey say they are being ethical, want to report in independent, detached ways, and avoid cheerleading. However, they are working in an industry in which there has been a substantial expansion by commercial and sports organisations, which are now dominating the field. As a result, sports journalists in Australia are operating in ethically grey areas at times, particularly when compared strictly with the MEAA (2020) Code of Ethics. This leads to questions over the relevance of the code, particularly with influence over commercial factors and dealing with sources from sports organisations, which impact on journalists' independence and honesty in reporting. It is also important to consider whether the greater influence of commercial interests and conflicts in sports reporting really matters in the context of the new environment. If audiences understand this is how the sports and sports journalism fields operate – and with the rise of club sites offering one-sided content, many fans do not appear to want critical analysis of their teams – then should sports journalism succumb to these forces and officially compromise on the traditional ethical guidelines? This book has argued for a greater focus on more independent reporting, free of the suffocating constraints of external commercial factors and the control of sports organisations. It is certainly the more difficult option and requires significant changes in gatekeeping at individual, routines and organisational levels. These shifts are essential in ensuring sports journalists and their newsrooms rebuild journalistic capital, which in turn could bring changes in economic capital.

One overarching area of focus needs to be delivering honest and independent reporting and commentary to audiences. This includes a greater concentration on critical aspects, and being less controlled by sanitised, media-managed appearances and statements delivered by sports organisations and their athletes. It also involves experimenting with different approaches to storytelling in order to ensure this vital part of the news media is able to survive and, perhaps, thrive again. Change is important by focusing on seeking greater diversity in content and sources – and less uniformity of content. Choosing to report in a more traditional way and aiming to produce more "pure" journalistic material instead of information tainted by the influence of external commercial and sports organisations is essential. Altering these approaches will be difficult, especially given the state of the industry with regard to staffing and financial levels, and the sports journalists' perceptions about the contemporary and future work environment. If some of the changes outlined are implemented, they will improve the quality of material being delivered, and provide greater public interest and entertainment benefits for audiences. Crucially, they can also help to ensure sports journalism regains a stronger place in the sports field instead of being a heavily dominated player.

6 Contemporary models of sports journalism

To conclude this analysis of Australian sports journalism this chapter advances the theory of sports journalism scholarship by outlining two preliminary conceptual models. The first involves the development of a typology of sports journalism, highlighting five types. The field of Australian sports journalism is then mapped, detailing amounts of journalistic and economic capital, as well as power, forces and threats. These contributions provide an important theoretical perspective on the many practical elements of the study, but it is essential to note they are limited to a sample of 120 sports journalists in mainstream, metropolitan newsrooms. While this represents approximately 20% of the industry, it is still relatively small and can impact the reliability of the results. Based on this exploratory analysis, the study provides opportunities for future research in other nations, and further advancing of the theoretical foundations of these conceptual models. Cross-national studies have provided rich data and detailed analysis in aspects of general journalism (see Hanitzsch 2011; Hanitzsch et al. 2020). Similar approaches could be applied to sports journalism and sports media to gain a greater understanding of the issues and perceptions in these highly consumed areas.

A typology of Australian sports journalism

Typologies have been utilised in other areas of journalism (for examples see Hanitzsch 2011; Hanitzsch & Vos 2018; Hanitzsch et al. 2020; Meyen & Riesmeyer 2012; Tandoc & Takahashi 2014; Weaver & Wilhoit 1996), but sport has not been a specific focus in these studies. As Tandoc and Takahashi (2014) argue, roles may differ across specialisations. Meyen and Riesmeyer (2012) state developing a typology has two aims: describing different types of behaviours and identifying factors that influence these types. This model outlines five dimensions developed from factors that influence Australian sports journalists. The types are: home focus, cheerleader, audience centric, personal reflector and critical watchdog.

To develop the typology, data from the 120 sports journalists was analysed from 36 items related to how important specific role descriptors were in their work (see examples from Tables 3.1, 3.2 and 6.1). In this part of the survey, some items were included from the Worlds of Journalism Study (2016), while some were adapted to contain a sport focus. Other items were added based on their theoretical or practical relevance to sports journalism. Responses were on a five-point Likert scale, ranging from extremely important (5) to unimportant (1). The 36 role descriptions were analysed in an exploratory factor analysis utilising SPSS 26 software. Eigen values of greater than 1.0 were employed to determine factors after they were rotated using Varimax with Kaiser Normalization. The item loadings for each factor were then assessed. Items with a loading greater than 0.5 were considered

Table 6.1 Exploratory factor analysis of sports journalist role descriptions

	Cheerleader	Home Focus	Audience Centric	Personal Reflector	Critical Watchdog
Satisfying athletes	0.783				
Satisfying your publication's advertisers	0.608				
Satisfying team media managers or PR staff	0.745				
Conveying a positive image of sports industry	0.652				
Being a cheerleader in your work	0.545				
Your home country losing		0.845			
Your home country winning		0.804			
Satisfying your audience			0.795		
Getting information to the public quickly			0.724		
Not missing a story			0.593		
Putting yourself into the story				0.864	
Using I, we and us in stories				0.779	
Being critical of players					0.820
Being critical of the home team					0.756
Eigenvalues	3.89	2.64	2.32	1.13	1.82
Percentage of variance explained	16.9	11.5	10.1	4.9	7.9
Crohnbach's Alpha	0.76	0.83	0.67	0.66	0.65

Note: Extraction Method: Principal Component Analysis; Rotation Method: Varimax with Kaiser Normalization

acceptable thresholds (Hair et al. 1998; Tabachnick & Fidell 2001). Crohn-bach's Alpha was used to assess reliability items for each factor. A reliable outcome is generally considered above $\alpha = .70$; however results above $\alpha = .50$ can be considered acceptable when undertaking work of an exploratory nature (Hair et al. 1998). This project is exploratory and none of the five dimensions exhibited at less than $\alpha = .65$.

The two strongest types, with high internal consistency, were home focus ($\alpha = .83$) and cheerleader ($\alpha = .76$). There were three marginally weaker factors: audience centric ($\alpha = .67$), personal reflector ($\alpha = .66$) and critical watchdog ($\alpha = .65$). While the exploratory factor analysis results support the individual factors described earlier, there are similarities between elements of these types, including home focus, cheerleader, audience centric and personal reflector. This suggests more of a subjective and entertainment focus to the work of Australian sports journalists in contemporary media than detached, traditional reporting.

Home focus

The home-focus type indicates the value of the home country and local teams in the perceptions of Australian sports journalists. This dimension included items relating to the importance of sports journalists' home country winning and home country losing in their work. A local focus has been noted in other research that combines some of these elements with aspects of cheerleading and promoting, such as reporters being described as "homers" (Billings et al. 2011; Hardin et al. 2009; Schultz 2005). While it suggests a more subjective perspective to match reporting, this type has differences to the cheerleader category in that these sports journalists do not necessarily cheer for the home team, even though their reports are angled towards it. Routines and organisational gatekeeping levels are also at play. Reporters are often assigned to a round and ultimately produce material about teams and nations that the audience wants to consume, and this local content is what the organisation is encouraging – or demanding. Entertainment and business considerations are crucial to these decisions, with a push for readership or ratings. There are also elements of national identity involved, with sport providing reflections of nations, national pride and stereotypes (see Billings et al. 2011; Boyle & Haynes 2009; Garland & Rowe 1999; Hutchins 2005; Hutchins & Rowe 2012; Vincent & Kian 2013). The focus on the home team winning or losing is closely related with the reporting of core sports (see English 2014b, 2017; Schultz-Jorgensen 2005). As mentioned in Chapter 2, journalists in the study discussed how their role was to "provide a mirror" to a nation "obsessed by sport". Stories on the local team or nation are more likely to be published or broadcast, and it is unsurprising these results are considered crucial to the journalists' perceptions. This classification has some similarities with the cheerleader type of sports journalist, and complements the audience-centric typology, with the information being published giving the audience what they want.

Cheerleader

Cheerleading has been a consistent criticism of sports journalists around the globe (see, for example, Boyle 2006; Boyle et al. 2012; English 2016a, 2017; Rowe 2007; Schultz-Jorgensen 2005) and it remains a feature of Australian sports journalism. In this type, the items were: being a cheerleader in your work, satisfying athletes, satisfying your publication's advertisers, satisfying team media managers or PR staff, and conveying a positive image of the sports industry. It is unsurprising that the cheerleader dimension is strong given the regular criticism, including from those involved in teams themselves. As mentioned in Chapter 2, Trevor Bayliss, a former England cricket coach, said Australian journalists do not criticise their own side (Dobell 2019). However, cheerleading can be a dirty word for many journalists, who in the survey commented regularly along the lines of it being important to be "a reporter, not a supporter". In contrast, there were elements of the "supporter" in reporting (see English 2017; Hardin 2005), which is evident through some respondents seeing themselves as promoters of sport. A television journalist noted it was a role to "give a voice to sport in a positive way". The cheerleader approach can involve overlooking negative elements in news. These aspects are in contrast to the traditional detached, ethical guidelines to journalism, but as mentioned have been associated historically with sports reporting. News choices reflect the individual level of gatekeeping, although they can also outline an organisational approach if the company encourages this type of writing and story angles. Again, these elements link with aspects of home focus, audience centric and personal reflector types in that there is a considerable subjective component to the work.

Audience centric

Traditionally, journalists have been told they are writing for the audience and this classification reflects this routine. The items included in this dimension were not missing a story, getting information to the public quickly and satisfying your audience in your work. This type can be located within individual, routines and organisational levels of gatekeeping, and is part of three slightly weaker classifications that emerged from the exploratory analysis.

It reflects the search for capital – particularly economic capital – in attracting or maintaining audience share to increase the product's value. Journalistic capital can also be impacted, with the level of "quality" content being a factor in determining a publication's place in the field. An upmarket title may pursue high-journalistic content while a tabloid may produce clickbait-style articles to lift ratings or hits. The audience-centric dimension aligns with the MEAA (2020) elements of informing and entertaining audiences, and highlights some key roles and routines. Reporters in this type reflect an entertainment approach and aspects such as lifting circulation by focusing on the sport section – or increasing audiences in broadcast or online (see Boyle 2017; Boyle & Haynes 2009; Hargreaves 1986; Horky & Stelzner 2013; Nicholson et al. 2015). Journalists noted the importance of informing the public "in a fair manner", satisfying the audience, and how breaking stories was a vital way of attracting and keeping audiences. One respondent, for example, saw the role of the sports journalist as taking "spectators to the sport". The audience-centric type can also lead to a home focus and subjective or cheerleading-style decisions in an attempt to provide the audience with the information it craves.

Personal reflector

Similar to cheerleading, personalisation and a subjective focus have been criticised in traditional journalistic reporting (see Anderson 2001; Billings et al. 2011; Boyle et al. 2012; Garrison & Salwen 1989; English 2018; Hardin 2005; Marchetti 2005; McEnnis 2016; Rowe 2004). Responses in the personal reflector classification related to the importance of using I, we and us in stories, and the journalist putting themselves into the story. While it is recognised that true objectivity or neutrality is out of reach and not expected by audiences (see Steen 2015; Ramon 2016; Weedon & Wilson 2017), personalisation, subjectivity and opinion in stories raise questions about independence and ethics, which are considered vital in other areas of journalism (see Boyle et al. 2012; Hardin 2005; Hardin et al. 2009; Mindich 1998; Rowe 2004; Schudson 2001; Tuchman 1972). Boyle et al. (2012) have argued there can be confusion about sports journalists' roles and note issues over balanced reporting (see also Hardin 2005). In this type, the subjective voice applies to individual and roles and routines levels around language choice, personal pronouns and the journalist's own experiences. This method conflicts with traditional independent and detached elements of journalism. Multiple respondents said a threat to sports journalism was "reporters thinking they have to have an opinion in stories", or they indicated "too much opinion" was undesirable. However, these characteristics are an important feature of journalists who operate as columnists or commentators, including ex-players, and it is their job to inject opinion and personalise their work. As one print-based columnist said: "What applies more to me, in my role in opinion, is to entertain." These aspects highlight some of the blurring that occurs between the roles of reporters, columnists and commentators. It is evident that these elements are associated with the cheerleader and audience-centric types, where the journalists apply subjective techniques in their storytelling.

Critical watchdog

Critical watchdog was the final dimension, reflecting the traditional aims of Fourth Estate journalism, including critical, detached and sceptical reporting (see Mindich 1998; Schudson 2001; Tuchman 1972). The items in this type involve perceptions of the journalists being critical of the home team, and being critical of players. This outlook often conflicts with the stronger cheerleader and home-focus classifications, as well as the personal reflector type. A lack of critical watchdog reporting has been mentioned throughout sports journalism's history (for examples see Boyle & Haynes 2009; Boyle et al. 2012; Hardin 2005; Hardin et al. 2009; Henningham 1995; Rowe 2004, 2007). Along with investigative pieces, watchdog journalism is not a consistent feature of the contemporary field, in part due to reduced budgets. Respondents talked regularly about the need for critical watchdog reporting by holding sport, clubs and athletes to account, or finding the stories the media departments "don't want you to know about". In this environment, journalists being able to do their job "without fear or favour" was considered important. Elements in this type include journalists not wanting to be public relation agents for players or clubs, and to uncover stories that clubs do not want published. One respondent said there was the need for "objective reporters rather than cheerleaders", while others said threats in Australian journalism came from "too many fans in the media" and "fans with typewriters". These comments are similar to complaints from international journalists (see Booth 2013; Keating 2001; Mitchell 2020). This classification has some links with the audience-centric type, with the sports journalist wanting to provide high-capital journalistic information, as well as entertaining and informing, which can increase economic capital.

Sports journalism and general journalism typologies

The typology of Australian sports journalism has some similarities with those developed in previous scholarship of general forms of journalism. However, there are elements specific to sports journalism. The cheerleader dimension has clear links with the opportunist facilitator (Hanitzsch 2011), promoters (Meyen & Riesmeyer 2012) and collaborative classifications (Hanitzsch et al. 2020). Hanitzsch (2011) states the opportunist facilitator supports official policies, conveys positive images of those in charge (see also Hanitzsch et al. 2020) and does not perceive their role as detached reporters. Meyen and Riesmeyer (2012) note promoters serve their audience but also business elements, such as advertising. They say journalists can aim to avoid damage with business partners, and be more aligned sometimes with marketing than journalism. The cheerleader as sports journalist promotes athletes, clubs, teams or nations, or works within frameworks that include broader commercial elements, or tie-ups with sports or corporate organisations. These descriptions are closely matched with previous scholarship, and in contrast to the traditional approach to journalistic reporting.

The audience-centric type shares similarities with Weaver and Wilhoit's (1996) disseminator, Hanitzsch's (2011) populist disseminator, Meyen and Riesmeyer's (2012) service providers and Hanitzsch et al.'s (2020) accommodative groupings. Hanitzsch (2011) notes the strong orientation towards the audience and attracting the biggest audience, while Hanitzsch et al. (2020) state these journalists see the audience members as consumers, wanting to provide them with news they can use. Meyen and Riesmeyer (2012) argue these journalists aim to fulfil the wishes of their audience and understand their demands. This close alignment towards the audience also contains elements of the home-focus and cheerleader classifications, with reporters attempting to provide the content the audience wants in informative and entertaining ways.

The critical watchdog type is comparable with the detached watchdogs (Hanitzsch 2011), the monitorial (Hanitzsch et al. 2020) and the critical-monitorial classifications (Hanitzsch & Vos 2018), as well as having similarities with the adversary role (Weaver & Wilhoit 1996). Hanitzsch (2011) notes how in most Western countries the detached approach dominates the journalistic field, which involves being watchdogs of government and business elites, and against the idea of supporting official policies (see also Hanitzsch & Vos 2018; Hanitzsch et al. 2020). This dominance is not at the same level in the Australian sports journalism field, where it is a somewhat weaker type. However, critical reporting still applies, although it is rarely argued that it occurs at the same intensity in sport as it does in other areas, such as political journalism.

There are less obvious similarities between the home-focus and personal reflector types. Weaver and Wilhoit's (1996) populist mobiliser has providing entertainment as one element, which links with the audience centric and home focus, but their other characteristics of setting the agenda or letting the public express views do not apply. Providing information that appeals most to the audience, such as nationally focused results, also contains elements of the accommodative approach outlined by Hanitzsch et al. (2020). However, these groupings are more closely related to the roles and routines of sports reporting, and therefore highlight some differences between this subfield and general journalism. As a result, original descriptions are required for the work undertaken by sports journalists in Australia.

The Australian sports journalism field

The mapping of the Australian sports journalism field (Figure 6.1) reflects the strong influence of commercial elements in contemporary media, with the majority of items situated towards the economic capital pole. Critical characteristics have been plotted based on responses of the journalists in the survey and conditions in the broader industry, based on journalistic and economic capital (see English 2016a). This has been undertaken as a theoretical exercise and been developed through analysis and estimation. By locating types of classifications, media, news and staff, it provides an understanding of the levels of capital and power, pressures and forces, and dominant and dominated actors within the field (see Bourdieu 1984, 1998). It is evident in the mapping that economic capital is the primary influence on organisations, media and journalistic roles (see Benson & Neveu 2005; Bourdieu 1998). In this design, journalistic capital, which includes elements of cultural and social capital, as well as power and prestige (see Hovden 2008; Meyen & Riesmeyer 2011; Vos et al. 2019), is combined with economic capital to determine total capital for the actors and agents (see also English 2016a).

To build on the typology of Australian sports journalism, the dimensions have been situated in the field. Most of the dimensions are located towards the economic pole, except for the critical watchdog classification, which contains high journalistic capital, through Fourth Estate-style reporting, investigations, and public-interest publishing. The audience-centric and home-focus types possess positive total capital, with their aims of giving consumers the information they desire, which helps with economic goals of lifting circulations, hits and broadcast figures. Both types allow for quality journalistic contributions, although the home focus can omit key information and angles about the "away" teams, and does not always highlight the most important details when straight or pure reporting is concerned. The personal reflector and cheerleader types have negative overall capital but positive economic capital. Cheerleading involves promoting the home team, satisfying key figures in teams or organisations, feeling part of the team, and operating as a "mouthpiece" for athletes or clubs. These roles raise crucial ethical issues and lead to low journalistic capital. The personal reflector type, which includes subjective reporting, experiences issues over balance, but also includes the legitimate roles of columnists and broadcasters providing opinion in conjunction with journalistic reporting, resulting in higher overall capital than cheerleaders.

The types of media appear in a greater range of areas, depending on their content and corporate focus. Commercial television and radio rely heavily on economic ambitions, in contrast to non-commercial broadcasters, such as the ABC, which pursue journalistic capital and undertake more "pure" and detached journalism, although there are budgetary elements in that the organisation has received less government funding over recent years. Television traditionally has a broader audience reach than radio, as well as paying more for sports rights and content (see ABC 2015; Fox Sports 2015; Letts 2018), and contains more overall capital, status and market dominance. In the survey, television journalists were most satisfied with job security and pay, again highlighting the strong commercial current in this part of the industry. Most news agencies provide "straight" reports of news for subscribers, earning some journalistic capital, but small amounts of economic capital. The low profile of this role, including in terms of power and prestige, contributes to the small overall amount of capital. For example, until talk of Australian Associated Press closing in 2020, few people outside of the nation's media understood the service agencies provided. Newspapers have been a declining force economically, but still provide the largest segment of sports journalists in the nation and often set the news agenda through print and online products. However, the overall status of newspapers is falling, particularly with the increase in digital platforms. Online media is predominantly aligned with entertainment and building larger audiences, but the pursuit of economic capital has been historically challenging and at times has damaged the quality of journalistic content. As discussed throughout the book, the sports journalism field is being impacted by two influential external forces in sports organisations and commercial factors. Commercial factors are represented through the positive economic capital pole and, while sports organisations themselves sit outside this field, they have become actors through some of their digital content. Despite operating primarily through commercial and public-relations aims, sports organisations do provide some journalistic value through their "reporting", although these contributions are by club journalists or media staff (see Mirer 2019; Sherwood et al. 2017a, 2017b). They also host content on their sites, allowing journalists to access press conferences and club details without having to travel.

In terms of roles, the positions with the largest amounts of overall capital are the sports editors, chiefs of staff or newsroom equivalent. As the dominant players in the newsroom, these figures determine the direction of the editorial coverage, within their organisational constraints and gatekeeping levels, including budget limitations. With a focus towards financial

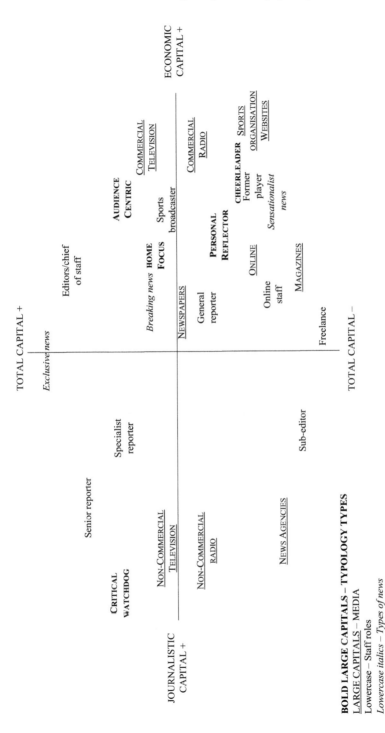

Figure 6.1 The Australian sports journalism field

BOLD LARGE CAPITALS – TYPOLOGY TYPES
LARGE CAPITALS – MEDIA
Lowercase – Staff roles
Lowercase italics – Types of news

elements and longer-term security, they are located more towards the economic pole. It is important to note this is a general guide and not reflective of all staff in these positions. Senior reporters and specialist reporters have high levels of journalistic capital, due to the cultural capital developed throughout their careers, and through their specific rounds and contacts (see Benson & Neveu 2005; English 2019). Senior reporters are also likely to have more autonomy, which can give them opportunities to say no to commercial influences, such as Baum's (2020) rejection of a Rafael Nadal interview subject to product placement. General reporters are the allrounders of the newsroom (see English 2019), with an emphasis on breaking news, but also driving traffic. Online staff can be more entertainment focused, with the intent of increasing readers and turning around content quickly, which is often repurposed from other sources, including sports organisations, and is rarely exclusive. In the study, online staff were the most overworked, and had the least satisfaction in the most categories, including pessimistic views over the future of the industry (see English 2019). Sub-editors own relatively moderate levels of journalistic capital, being the safety net of newsrooms due to roles of verification and ensuring accuracy, but as one of the first areas to be cut when savings need to be made, they possess low economic capital. Former players, who are predominantly hired in broadcast commentary roles, were shown in Chapter 2 to have a stronger cheerleading focus in the survey, as well as being accused by sports journalists of being a threat to the industry, having no training and "hijacking the jobs" of "experienced journalists". Sports broadcasters can also fit into these categories although, like senior reporters, they have developed cultural capital and status while combining reporting and commentary that can include critical elements as well as praise. At the negative end of total capital are freelancers, who like sub-editors have been seen by management as being dispensable, and in this dominated position rely on the organisation hiring them and often controlling their direction.

Briefly, the type of content with the most total capital is exclusive news. It contains the highest levels of journalistic capital, is the hardest to get, fulfils the traditional aims of Fourth Estate reporting, and is also utilised to drive traffic and build audiences (see Bourdieu 1998; English 2014a). As a print reporter said in Chapter 2, "the biggest influence" was exclusive stories. Breaking news is also important, although it possesses less journalistic capital than in previous eras as the information is shared so quickly online. Further, it is often released by sports organisations and is second-hand by the time the story is produced by journalists. Sensationalist news and clickbait are attempts at driving the most traffic and clicks, but while they build economic capital they contain little journalistic capital, particularly through a traditional reporting lens.

Power, control and threats in a time of crisis

Power, control and threats have been key themes throughout this book. Through the mapping of the Australian sports journalism field and the development of the typology of Australian sports journalism, these elements have been discussed in relation to forces, pressures and dominance to provide a greater understanding of the industry. In this exploratory analysis, the conceptual typology has illustrated key classifications of sports journalism, highlighting the perceived influences of sports journalists in their work. While the area is being dominated in the sports media field (see Figure 6.1), the mapping indicates the power of sports organisations and commercial factors in the sports journalism field. However, this is not the whole story of the field, with the typology, media, staff roles and news types also operating as forces within this complex space. These preliminary conceptual models provide valuable additions to scholarship, helping to guide current sports journalists as they position themselves for the future, and assisting educators in highlighting some of the requirements needed by students dreaming of entering the industry. Combined with the comments from the journalists throughout the book, these discussions are particularly important as Australian sports journalism attempts to navigate a time of crisis, build its journalistic and economic capital, retain its relevance, and regain its reputation as a dominant player.

References

ABC 2015, 'NRL signs mega TV deal, Fox Sports gets rights to Saturday fixture', 26 November, viewed 17 November 2019, <https://www.abc.net.au/news/2015-11-26/nrl-tv-deal/6976996>.

ABC 2019, 'James Faulkner, Australian cricketer, says social media posts implying he had a boyfriend were a "misunderstanding"', 30 April, viewed 1 May 2019, <https://www.abc.net.au/news/2019-04-30/james-faulkner-says-relationship-announcement-a-misunderstanding/11057352#:~:text=On%20Monday%20night%20Faulkner%20posted,togetherfor5years%22%20on%20Twitter%20and%20Instagram>.

ABS 2020, *Population Clock*, Australian Bureau of Statistics, <https://www.abs.gov.au/AUSSTATS/abs@.nsf/Web+Pages/Population+Clock?opendocument&ref=HPKI>.

ACCC 2019, *Digital Platforms Inquiry Final Report*, the Australian Competition and Consumer Commission, viewed 3 October 2019, <https://www.accc.gov.au/publications/digital-platforms-inquiry-final-report>.

ACCC Digital Platforms Inquiry 2018, *Media, Entertainment and Arts Alliance submission to the Australian Competition and Consumer Commission's Digital Platforms Inquiry*, <https://www.accc.gov.au/system/files/Media%2C%20Entertainment%20and%20Arts%20Alliance%20%28April%202018%29.pdf>.

AFLW 2019, *AFLW Collective Bargaining Agreement*, <https://resources.afl.com.au/afl/document/2019/12/04/cf315c0d-6100-4a06-ab3b-d42d96407032/AFLW-CBA-Nov2019.pdf>.

The Age 2003, '3AK's sporting chance', 14 April, viewed 11 November 2019, <https://www.theage.com.au/entertainment/tv-and-radio/3aks-sporting-chance-20031204-gdwv0a.html>.

The Age 2004, 'Gnome slur angers Langer', 16 February, viewed 12 December 2019, <https://www.theage.com.au/sport/cricket/gnome-slur-angers-langer-20040216-gdxbei.html>.

Anderson, W 2001, 'Does the cheerleading ever stop? Major League Baseball and sports journalism', *Journalism and Mass Communication Quarterly*, vol. 78, no. 2, pp. 355–382.

Andrewes, F 2000, 'They play in your home: Cricket, media and modernity in pre-war Australia', in J Mangan & J Nauright (eds), *Sport in Australasian Society*, Frank Cass Publishers, London, pp. 93–110.

AthletesVoice 2020, 'About *AthletesVoice*', viewed 5 February 2020, <https://www.athletesvoice.com.au/about/>.

Baum, G 2020, 'Strings attached: There is no sport like tennis for selling its soul', *The Age*, 17 January, viewed 19 January 2020, <https://www.theage.com.au/sport/tennis/strings-attached-there-is-no-sport-like-tennis-for-selling-its-soul-20200117-p53scg.html>.

BBC 2016, 'Michael Vaughan: Ex-England captain denies "agenda" claims by Jonathan Trott', 22 September, viewed 10 November 2019, <https://www.bbc.com/sport/cricket/37436404>.

Benson, R & Neveu, E (eds) 2005, *Bourdieu and the Journalistic Field*, Polity Press, Cambridge.

Berry, S 2020, 'How cricket has changed in my 43 years touring with England', *The Daily Telegraph*, 28 January, viewed 29 January 2020, <https://www.telegraph.co.uk/cricket/2020/01/28/scyld-berry-cricket-has-changed-44-years-touring-england/>.

Billings, A 2019, 'Panel chair comments', *International Forum on Sports Communication*, Chengdu Sport University, Chengdu, China, 15–17 November.

Billings, A, Angelini, J & Wu, D 2011, 'Nationalistic notions of the superpowers: Comparative analyses of the American and Chinese telecasts in the 2008 Beijing Olympiad', *Journal of Broadcasting & Electronic Media*, vol. 55, no. 2, pp. 251–266.

Blackiston, H 2020, 'Foxtel cuts 200 jobs, stands down 140 team members as it "accelerates transformation"', *Mumbrella*, 9 April 2020, viewed 3 May 2020, <https://mumbrella.com.au/foxtel-cuts-200-jobs-stands-down-140-team-members-as-it-accelerates-transformation-624248>.

Blake, M 2012, 'A sporting career', *The Age*, 1 October, viewed 4 February 2020, <https://www.theage.com.au/sport/a-sporting-career-20121001-26v4m.html>.

Booth, L 2013, 'Boxing clever', *The Nightwatchman*, pp. 4–9, viewed 8 August 2014, <http://www.thenightwatchman.net/wp-content/uploads/2013/06/The%20Nightwatchman%20-%20Issue%202%20-%20Sample%20edition.pdf>.

Bourdieu, P 1984, *Distinction*, Harvard University Press, Cambridge, MA.

Bourdieu, P 1998, *On Television and Journalism*, Pluto Press, London.

Bourdieu, P 2005, 'The political field, the social science field, and the journalistic field', in R Benson & E Neveu (eds), *Bourdieu and the Journalistic Field*, Polity Press, Cambridge, pp. 29–47.

Boyle, R 2006, *Sports Journalism: Context and Issues*, Sage, London.

Boyle, R 2017, 'Sports journalism', *Digital Journalism*, vol. 5, no. 5, pp. 493–495.

Boyle, R & Haynes, R 2009, *Power Play: Sport, the Media and Popular Culture*, 2nd edn, Edinburgh University Press, Edinburgh.

Boyle, R, Rowe, D & Whannel, G 2012, '"Delight in Trivial Controversy"? Questions for sports journalism', in S Allan (ed), *The Routledge Companion to News and Journalism*, revised edn, Routledge, Abingdon and Oxfordshire, pp. 245–255.

Breed, W 1955, 'Social control in the newsroom: A functional analysis', *Social Forces*, vol. 34, no. 4, pp. 326–335.

Cashman, R 1995, *Paradise of Sport: The Rise of Organised Sport in Australia*, Oxford University Press, Melbourne.

Coward, M 2015, 'It long irked me that sports writing, in this country, has been devalued', *ASC Lifetime Achievement Award: 2015*, viewed 30 November 2019, <https://speakola.com/sports/mike-coward-asc-lifetime-achievement-2015>.

Curtis, B 2020, 'Locked out: How the coronavirus could change American sports-writing forever', *The Ringer*, viewed 11 March 2020, <https://www.theringer.com/2020/3/10/21173499/coronavirus-locker-room-mlb-nba-nfl-sportswriting>.

Dalton, T 2017, 'What's eating Rabbits?', *The Weekend Australian*, 1 July, viewed 1 July 2017, <https://www.theaustralian.com.au/life/weekend-australian-magazine/whats-eating-rabbits-sports-commentator-ray-warren/news-story/c8351698bc651a359d8d9079aed9e022?utm_content=SocialFlow&utm_campaign=EditorialSF&utm_source=TheAustralian&utm_medium=Twitter>.

Davis, G 2020, 'Going all out for Kayo', *The Sunday Mail*, 1 March, p. 93.

Deuze, M 2007, *Media Work*, Polity Press, Cambridge.

Dobell, G 2019, 'I'm a player, really: I think I understand how players think', *The Cricket Monthly*, viewed 19 September 2019, <http://www.thecricketmonthly.com/story/1201043/-i-m-a-player-really-i-think-i-understand-how-players-think?appsrc=cricinfo>.

Doran, M 2020, 'News Corp to cut jobs in restructure towards digital-only community and regional newspapers', *ABC*, 28 May, viewed 6 June 2020, <https://www.abc.net.au/news/2020-05-28/news-corp-to-cut-jobs-in-restructure-towards-digital-newspapers/12294970>.

Edmund, S 2019, 'Caleb Ewan is primed to fire in a Tour de France debut he says is long overdue', *Sunday Herald Sun*, 15 June, viewed 16 June 2019, <https://www.heraldsun.com.au/sport/more-sports/cycling/caleb-ewan-is-primed-to-fire-in-a-tour-de-france-debut-he-says-is-long-overdue/news-story/df72c5569d0bf8120c589aaaf2202518>.

English, P 2010, 'Newspapers versus the web: How news organisations use their news in print and online', Honours thesis, University of the Sunshine Coast.

English, P 2013, 'Sports journalism's relationship with sport's corporate sector: A comparison between Australia, India and the United Kingdom', *Australian Journalism Review*, vol. 35, no. 2, pp. 47–57.

English, P 2014a, 'The same old stories: Exclusive news and uniformity of content in sports coverage', *International Journal of Sport Communication*, vol. 7, pp. 477–494.

English, P 2014b, 'Sports coverage in print and web newspapers: How online journalism has changed sports journalism', PhD thesis, University of the Sunshine Coast.

English, P 2016a, 'Mapping the sports journalism field: Bourdieu and broadsheet newsrooms', *Journalism*, vol. 17, no. 8, pp. 1001–1017.

English, P 2016b, 'New rules of the game: Sports journalism and profiles', in S Joseph & R Keeble (eds), *Profile Pieces and the "Human Interest" Bias*, Routledge, London, pp. 195–208.

English, P 2016c, 'Big business blurs sport journalism's critical eye', in G Sweeney (ed), *Global Corruption Report: Sport*, Taylor & Francis, London, pp. 347–351.

English, P 2017, 'Cheerleaders or critics? Australian and Indian sports journalists in the contemporary age', *Digital Journalism*, vol. 5, no. 5, pp. 532–548.

English, P 2018, 'Sports journalism', in J Nussbaum (ed), *Oxford Research Encyclopedia of Communication*, Oxford University Press, Oxford, <http://dx.doi.org/10.1093/acrefore/9780190228613.013.873>.

English, P 2019, 'State of play: A survey of sports journalists in Australia', *Australian Journalism Review*, vol. 41, no. 2, pp. 155–167.

English, P, Calder, A, Pearce, S & Kirby, K 2019, 'A new sporting horizon: a content analysis of Super Netball newspaper coverage', *Media International Australia*, vol. 171, no. 1, pp. 110–24.

Farrington, N, Kilvington, D, Saeed, A & Price, J 2012, *Race, Racism and Sports Journalism*, Routledge, London.

Fisher, C, Park, S, Young Lee, J, Fuller, G & Sang, Y 2019, *Digital News Report: Australia 2019*, News and Media Research Centre, Canberra, <http://dx.doi.org/10.25916/5cff18510a051>.

Fox Sports 2015, 'AFL $2.508 billion broadcast rights deal stacks up well with other sports, leagues worldwide', 19 August, 17 November 2019, <https://www.foxsports.com.au/afl/afl-2508-billion-broadcast-rights-deal-stacks-up-well-with-other-sports-leagues-worldwide/news-story/934466dae31b486ab31240089 88734fc>.

Garland, J & Rowe, M 1999, 'War minus the shooting? Jingoism, the English press, and Euro '96', *Journal of Sport & Social Issues*, vol. 23, no. 1, pp. 80–95.

Garrison, B & Salwen, M 1989, 'Newspaper sports journalists: A profile of the "profession"', *Journal of Sport and Social Issues*, vol. 13, no. 2, pp. 57–68.

Gleeson, M & Niall, J 2020, 'AFL, clubs stand down almost entire workforce on horrendous day for football', *The Age*, 28 March, viewed 24 March 2020, <https://www.theage.com.au/sport/afl/suns-football-department-staff-stood-down-indefinitely-20200323-p54cxb.html>.

Goldlust, J 1987, *Playing for Keeps*, Longman Cheshire, Melbourne.

The Guardian 2018, 'Marvel-lous idea? Etihad stadium renamed after Walt Disney deal', 24 May, viewed 31 October 2019, <https://www.theguardian.com/sport/2018/may/24/marvel-ous-entertainment-etihad-stadium-re-named-after-walt-disney-deal>.

Guinness, R 2011, *What a Ride: An Aussie Pursuit of the Tour de France*, 2nd edn, Allen & Unwin, Crows Nest.

Hair, J, Anderson, R, Tatham, R & Black, W 1998, *Multivariate Data Analysis*, Prentice Hall, Upper Saddle River, US.

Hallin, D & Mancini, P 2004, *Comparing Media Systems: Three Models of Media and Politics*, Cambridge University Press, Cambridge.

Hamilton, J 2004, *All the News That's Fit to Sell: How the Market Transforms Information Into News*, Princeton University Press, Princeton.

Hanitzsch, T 2011, 'Populist disseminators, detached watchdogs, critical change agents and opportunist facilitators: Professional milieus, the journalistic field and autonomy in 18 countries', *International Communication Gazette*, vol. 73, no. 6, pp. 477–494.

Hanitzsch, T, Hanusch, F, Mellado, C, Anikina, M, Berganza, R, Cangoz, I, Coman, M, Hamada, B, Hernández, M, Karadjov, C, Moreira, S, Mwesige, P, Plaisance, P, Reich, Z, Seethaler, J, Skewes, E, Noor, D & Yuen, EKW 2010, 'Mapping journalistic cultures across nations', *Journalism Studies*, vol. 12, no. 3, pp. 273–293.

Hanitzsch, T & Vos, T 2018, 'Journalism beyond democracy: A new look into journalistic roles in political and everyday life', *Journalism*, vol. 19, no. 2, pp. 146–164.

Hanitzsch, T, Vos, T, Standaert, O, Hanusch, F, Hovden, JF, Hermans, L & Ramaprasad, J 2020, 'Role orientations: Journalists' views on their place in society', in T Hanitzsch, F Hanusch, J Ramaprasad & A de Beer (eds), *Worlds of Journalism: Journalistic Cultures Around the Globe*, Columbia University Press, New York.

Hanusch, F 2015, 'A different breed altogether?', *Journalism Studies*, vol. 16, no. 6, pp. 816–833.

Hanusch, F & Bruns, A 2017, 'Journalistic branding on Twitter', *Digital Journalism*, vol. 5, no. 1, pp. 26–43.

Hardin, M 2005, 'Survey finds boosterism, freebies remain problem for newspaper sports departments', *Newspaper Research Journal*, vol. 26, no. 1, pp. 66–72.

Hardin, M, Zhong, B & Whiteside, E 2009, 'Sports coverage: "Toy department" or public-service journalism? The relationship between reporters' ethics and attitudes toward the profession', *International Journal of Sport Communication*, vol. 2, pp. 319–339.

Hargreaves, J 1986, *Sport, Power and Culture*, Polity Press, Cambridge.

Harman, J 2019, 'The changing art of cricket commentary', *Wisden Cricket Monthly*, 27 November, viewed 27 November 2019, <https://www.theguardian.com/sport/2019/nov/27/changing-art-cricket-commentary>.

Harris, B 2020, 'Rugby Australia's financial pain felt widely but not shared universally', *The Guardian*, 2 June, viewed 2 June 2020, <https://www.theguardian.com/sport/2020/jun/02/rugby-australias-financial-pain-felt-widely-but-not-shared-universally>.

Henningham, J 1995, 'A profile of Australian sports journalists', *The ACHPER Healthy Lifestyles Journal*, vol. 42, no. 3, pp. 13–17.

Henningham, J 1998, 'Australian journalists', in D Weaver (ed), *The Global Journalist*, Hampton Press, Cresskill, NJ, pp. 91–108.

Holt, O 2019, 'Athletics is dying and yet people like Paula Radcliffe and Lord Coe blame . . . Gabby Logan', *Daily Mail*, 6 October, viewed 25 November 2019, <https://www.dailymail.co.uk/sport/othersports/article-7541825/Athletics-dying-people-like-Paula-Radcliffe-Lord-Coe-blame-Gabby-Logan.html>.

Hooper, C 2014, 'Game, cheque, match', *The Age*, 25 January, viewed 3 February 2020, <https://www.smh.com.au/sport/tennis/game-cheque-match-20140120-313cs.html>.

Horky, T & Nieland, J-U 2013, *International Sports Press Survey 2011: Quantity and Quality of Sports Reporting*, Books on Demand, Norderstet.

Horky, T & Stelzner, B 2013, 'Sports reporting and journalistic principles', in P Pedersen (ed), *Routledge Handbook of Sport Communication*, Routledge, Abingdon and Oxfordshire, pp. 118–127.

Hovden, J 2008, 'Profane and sacred: A study of the Norwegian journalistic field', PhD thesis, University of Bergen, Norway.

Hutchins, B 2005, 'Unity, difference and the "national game": Cricket and Australian national identity', in S Wagg (ed), *Cricket and National Identity in the Postcolonial Age*, Routledge, London, pp. 9–27.

Hutchins, B & Boyle, R 2017, 'A community of practice', *Digital Journalism*, vol. 5, no. 5, pp. 496–512.

Hutchins, B & Rowe, D 2012, *Sport beyond Television: The internet, Digital Media and the Rise of Networked Media Sport*, Routledge, New York.

Jackson, R 2017, 'Melbourne's sports talk radio boom: Is anyone actually listening?', *The Guardian*, 14 April, viewed 11 November 2019, <https://www.theguardian. com/tv-and-radio/2017/apr/14/melbournes-sports-talk-radio-boom-is-anyone-actually-listening>.

Jackson, R (ed) 2019, *Electrifying 80s: Footy's Outrageous Decade in the Words of Its Best Writers*, The Slattery Media Group, Melbourne.

Karlsson, M 2011, 'The immediacy of online news, the visibility of journalistic processes and a restructuring of journalistic authority', *Journalism*, vol. 12, no. 3, pp. 279–295.

Keating, F 2001, 'These Australians the best ever? Stark raving lunacy', *The Guardian*, 30 July, viewed 30 June 2014, <http://www.theguardian.com/sport/2001/jul/30/comment>.

Keoghan, S, Phillips, S & Chammas, M 2020, 'In shock: Multiple clubs stand down staff in one of NRL's darkest days', *The Sydney Morning Herald*, 25 March, viewed 25 March 2020, <https://www.smh.com.au/sport/nrlin-shock-multiple-clubs-stand-down-staff-in-one-of-nrl-s-darkest-days-20200325-p54dw5.html>.

Kimmage, P 2020, 'Rory revisited: No question off limits, no subject out of bounds as Paul Kimmage meets golfer of the decade', *Irish Independent*, 2 February, viewed 3 February 2020, <https://www.independent.ie/sport/golf/rory-revisited-no-question-off-limits-no-subject-out-of-bounds-as-paul-kimmage-meets-golfer-of-the-decade-38918652.html>.

Kitson, R 2020, 'Murrayfield atmosphere reflected rising noise, bile and spite in rugby union', *The Guardian*, 11 February, viewed 12 February 2020, <https://www.theguardian.com/sport/2020/feb/11/murrayfield-atmosphere-rising-noise-bile-spite-rugby-union-six-nations-england-scotland>.

Knox, D 2019, 'Dennis Cometti inducted into the Sport Australia Hall of Fame', *TVTonight*, 12 October, viewed 7 November 2019, <https://tvtonight.com.au/2019/10/dennis-cometti-inducted-into-the-sport-australia-hall-of-fame.html>.

Knox, M 2020, 'McArdle sacking just the latest tick of rugby's doomsday clock', *The Sydney Morning Herald*, 24 January, viewed 24 January 2020, <https://www.smh.com.au/sport/rugby-union/mcardle-sacking-just-the-latest-tick-of-rugby-s-doomsday-clock-20200124-p53uee.html>.

Kruger, C 2019, 'News Corp seals Foxtel debt deal as it posts $306m loss', *The Sydney Morning Herald*, 8 November, viewed 8 November 2019, <https://www.smh.com.au/business/companies/news-corp-posts-306m-loss-blaming-sluggish-australian-economy-20191107-p538el.html>.

Lalor, P 2018, 'Players have their oval office bugged in appeal to audiences with attention deficit disorder', *The Australian*, 20 December, p. 24.

Lalor, P 2020a, 'D-Day as Cricket Australia walks tightrope', *The Australian*, 3 June, viewed 3 June 2020, <https://www.theaustralian.com.au/sport/cricket/dday-as-cricket-australia-walks-tightrope/news-story/28da606a7cc6e2f11150019a5ed25638>.

Lalor, P 2020b, 'Homophobia wins as officials dodge issue', *The Australian*, 15 January, viewed 15 January 2020, <https://www.theaustralian.com.au/sport/cricket/homophobia-wins-as-officials-dodge-issue/news-story/8c985f8c8eda71987de8ec878a19e4f3>.

Lawe-Davies, C & Le Brocque, R 2006, 'What's news in Australia?', in P Shoemaker & A Cohen (eds), *News Around the World*, Routledge, New York, pp. 93–118.

Lemon, G 2015, 'Just not cricket: How channel nine is destroying a legacy', *The Guardian*, 13 February, viewed 13 February 2015, <https://www.theguardian.com/sport/blog/2015/feb/13/channel-nine-destroying-cricket-legacy>.

Letts, S 2018, 'Seven and Foxtel win TV rights battle for cricket, but deal faces significant regulatory hurdles', *ABC*, 13 April, viewed 17 November 2019, <https://www.abc.net.au/news/2018-04-13/cricket-coverage-shakeup-with-seven-and-foxtel-winning-rights/9652964>.

Magnay, J & Halloran, J 2020, 'Olympic sports face big funding cuts after Tokyo 2020 Olympics', *The Australian*, 14 February, viewed 14 February 2020, <https://www.theaustralian.com.au/sport/olympics/olympic-sports-face-big-funding-cuts-after-tokyo-2020-olympics/news-story/c5930c74035c2d78508960d4204d0a2a>.

Marchetti, D 2005, 'Subfields of specialised journalism', in R Benson & E Neveu (eds), *Bourdieu and the Journalistic Field*, Polity Press, Cambridge, pp. 64–84.

Margaret Gee's Australian Media Guide 2018, 'Information Australia-Margaret Gee Media Group', <http://www.connectweb.com.au/search.aspx>.

Mason, E 2000, 'Why is sports journalism an oxymoron?', paper presented to *Conference 2000: Sports Journalism, Journalism Education Association of New Zealand Annual Conference*, University of Canterbury, Christchurch, viewed 14 October 2011, <http://www.jeanz.org.nz/Conference%20Papers%20-%20sports%20oxymoron.htm>.

Mason, W 2020, 'John McEnroe, Martina Navratilova want to tell Australians what's right and wrong with Margaret Court protest', *The Australian*, 30 January, viewed 30 January 2020, <https://www.theaustralian.com.au/sport/tennis/john-mcenroe-martina-navratilova-want-to-tell-australians-whats-right-and-wrong-with-margaret-court-protest/news-story/3c279d2947907aef1b408b359fc919a0>.

Masters, R 2020, 'Telcos' face-off in RA rights war a new kind of super league', *The Sydney Morning Herald*, 19 February, viewed 19 February 2020, <https://www.smh.com.au/sport/rugby-union/telcos-face-off-in-ra-rights-war-a-new-kind-of-super-league-20200218-p541xb.html>.

Mayer, H 1964, *The Press in Australia*, Lansdowne Press, Melbourne.

McChesney, R 1989, 'Media made sport: A history of sports coverage in the United States', in L Wenner (ed), *Media, Sport, and Society*, Sage, Newbury Park, CA, pp. 49–70.

McCulloch, I 2019, 'Botham says brace for abuse, but Ali urges fans to give Smith, Warner fair go', *Australian Associated Press*, 22 May, viewed 23 May 2019, <https://www.smh.com.au/sport/cricket/i-just-hope-they-get-treated-decently-ali-urges-fans-to-give-smith-warner-fair-go-20190522-p51pv6.html>.

McEnnis, S 2016, 'Following the action: How live bloggers are reimagining the professional ideology of sports journalism', *Journalism Practice*, vol. 10, no. 8, pp. 967–982.

McEnnis, S 2018, 'Toy department within the toy department? Online sports journalists and professional legitimacy', *Journalism*, 3 September, pp.1–17. DOI:10.1177/1464884918797613.

McEnnis, S 2019, 'A whole new ball game: How Sky Sports News journalists are learning from the academy', *Australian Journalism Review*, vol. 41, no. 2, pp. 197–209.

MEAA 2020, *Media Entertainment and Arts Alliance Code of Ethics*, viewed 2 February, <http://www.alliance.org.au/code-of-ethics.html>.

Meyen, M & Riesmeyer, C 2012, 'Service providers, sentinels, and traders', *Journalism Studies*, vol. 13, no. 3, pp. 386–401.

Miller, T, Lawrence, G, McKay, J & Rowe, D 2007, 'Global sport media', in A Tomlinson (ed), *The Sports Studies Reader*, Routledge, Abingdon and Oxford.

Mindich, D 1998, *Just the Facts: How "Objectivity" Came to Define American Journalism*, New York University Press, New York.

Mirer, M 2018, '"I did what I do" versus "I cover football": Boundary work, in-house media and athlete protest', *Journalism Practice*, vol. 12, no. 3, pp. 251–267.

Mirer, M 2019, 'Playing to the crowd: The audience's role in team-operated media', *Australian Journalism Review*, vol. 41, no. 2, pp. 183–195.

Mitchell, K 2020, 'Australian Open 2020: The tournament that tarnished tennis's image', *The Guardian*, 3 February, viewed 4 February 2020, <https://www.theguardian.com/sport/2020/feb/03/australian-open-2020-tournament-tarnished-tennis-image>.

National Union of Journalists 2019, *NUJ Code of Conduct*, viewed 6 August, <https://www.nuj.org.uk/about/nuj-code/>.

News.com.au 2020, 'Tennis Australia respond following John McEnroe and Martina Navratilova's on-court protest', 29 January, viewed 29 January 2020, <https://www.news.com.au/sport/tennis/australian-open/tennis-australia-respond-following-john-mcenroe-and-martina-navratilovas-oncourt-protest/news-story/cca43cfcc4756b099937b3fc9fb62e52>.

Nguyen, A 2008, *The Penetration of Online News*, VDM Publishing, Saarbrücken.

Nicholson, M, Kerr, A & Sherwood, M 2015, *Sport and the Media: Managing the Nexus*, 2nd edn, Routledge, London.

Nicholson, M, Zion, L & Lowden, D 2011, 'A profile of Australian sports journalists (revisited)', *Media International Australia*, vol. 140, pp. 84–96.

Obijiofor, L & Hanusch, F 2011, *Journalism across Cultures: An Introduction*, Palgrave MacMillan, Basingstoke.

O'Donnell, P, Zion, L & Sherwood, M 2016, 'Where do journalists go after newsroom job cuts?', *Journalism Practice*, vol. 10, no. 1, pp. 35–51.

Picard, R 2004, 'Commercialisation and newspaper quality', *Newspaper Research Journal*, vol. 25, no. 1, pp. 54–65.

Press Council of India 2018, 'Norms of journalistic conduct', viewed 8 November 2019, <http://presscouncil.nic.in/WriteReadData/userfiles/file/NORMS.pdf>.

Ramon, X 2016, 'Sports journalism ethics and quality of information: The coverage of the London 2012 Olympics in the British, American and Spanish press', PhD thesis, Universitat Pompeu Fabra, Departament de Comunicació, <https://www.tdx.cat/handle/10803/393739>.

Robinson, G 2020, 'No regrets': Hooper responds to gag claims on Folau sacking', *The Sydney Morning Herald*, 27 February, viewed 27 February 2020, <https://www.smh.com.au/sport/rugby-union/no-regrets-hooper-responds-to-gag-claims-on-folau-sacking-20200227-p544uk.html>.

Ronay, B 2019, 'Sebastian Coe's stance on Salazar displays a very British hypocrisy', *The Guardian*, 4 October, viewed 25 November 2019, <https://www.theguardian.com/sport/2019/oct/04/sebastian-coe-alberto-salazar-very-british-hypocrisy-athletics viewed>.

Rowe, D 2004, *Sport, Culture and the Media*, 2nd edn, Open University Press, Maidenhead.

Rowe, D 2007, 'Still the "toy department" of the news media?', *Journalism*, vol. 8, no. 4, pp. 385–405.

Sawai, A 2017, 'Harsha Bhogle unplugged: Candid truths on BCCI sack, Big B, insecurity in cricket', *The Economic Times*, 23 January, viewed 15 November 2019, <https://economictimes.indiatimes.com/magazines/panache/harsha-bhogle-unplugged-candid-truths-on-bcci-sack-big-b-insecurity-in-cricket/articleshow/56724924.cms?utm_source=contentofinterest&utm_medium=text&utm_campaign=cppst>.

Schudson, M 2001, 'The objectivity norm in American journalism', *Journalism*, vol. 2, no. 2, pp. 149–170.

Schultz, B 2005, *Sports Media: Planning, Production and Reporting*, Focal Press, Burlington.

Schultz-Jorgensen, S 2005, 'The world's best advertising agency: The sports press', *The House of Monday Morning*, 31 October, viewed 12 November 2011, <http://www.playthegame.org/upload//Sport_Press_Survey_English.pdf>.

Sherry, E, Osborne, A & Nicholson, M 2016, 'Images of sports women: A review', *Sex Roles*, vol. 74, no. 7–8, pp. 299–309.

Sherwood, M 2019, 'Citizen journalists, sports fans or advocates? The motivations of female independent sports media producers in Australia', *Australian Journalism Review*, vol. 41, no. 2, pp. 169–182.

Sherwood, M, Nicholson, M & Marjoribanks, T 2017a, 'Controlling the message and the medium?', *Digital Journalism*, vol. 5, no. 5, pp. 513–531.

Sherwood, M, Nicholson, M & Marjoribanks, T 2017b, 'Access, agenda building and information subsidies: Media relations in professional sport', *International Review for the Sociology of Sport*, vol. 52, no. 8, pp. 992–1007.

Sherwood, M & O'Donnell, P 2018, 'Once a journalist, always a journalist?', *Journalism Studies*, vol. 19, no. 7, pp. 1021–1038.

Sherwood, M, Osborne, A, Nicholson, M & Sherry, E 2017c, 'Newswork, news values, and audience considerations: Factors that facilitate media coverage of women's sports', *Communication & Sport*, vol. 5, no. 6, pp. 647–668.

Sherwood, M & English, P 2019, 'New boundaries and perspectives in sports journalism', *Australian Journalism Review*, vol. 41, no. 2, pp. 151–4.

Shoemaker, P & Cohen, A (eds) 2006, *News Around the World*, Routledge, New York.

Shoemaker, P & Vos, T 2009, *Gatekeeping Theory*, Routledge, New York.

Singer, J 2010, 'Journalism ethics amid structural change', *Dædalus*, vol. 139, no. 2, pp. 89–99.

Society of Professional Journalists 2019, *SPJ Code of Ethics*, viewed 2 February, <https://www.spj.org/ethicscode.asp>.

Steen, R 2008, *Sports Journalism: A Multimedia Primer*, Routledge, London.

Steen, R 2011, 'Rose-tinted spectacle? The view from the pressbox', in J Sudgen & A Tomlinson (eds), *Watching the Olympics: Politics, Power and Representation*, Routledge, London, pp. 213–227.

Steen, R 2015, *Sports Journalism: A multimedia primer, 2nd edn,* Routledge, London.

Stoddart, B 1986, *Saturday Afternoon Fever,* Angus and Robertson Publishers, North Ryde.

Suggs, D 2016, 'Tensions in the press box: Understanding relationships among sports media and source organizations', *Communication & Sport,* vol. 4, no. 3, pp. 261–281.

The Sydney Morning Herald 2003, 'Lehmann sorry for racial slur', 17 January, viewed 12 December 2019, <https://www.smh.com.au/sport/cricket/lehmann-sorry-for-racial-slur-20030117-gdg4d9.html>.

Tabachnick, B & Fidell, L 2001, 'Principal components and factor analysis', in B Tabachnick & L Fidell (eds), *Using Multivariate Statistics,* Allyn & Bacon, Boston, pp. 582–652.

Tandoc, E, Hellmueller, L & Vos, T 2013, 'Mind the gap', *Journalism Practice,* vol. 7, no. 5, pp. 539–554.

Tandoc, E & Takahashi, B 2014, 'Playing a crusader role or just playing by the rules? Role conceptions and role inconsistencies among environmental journalists', *Journalism,* vol. 15, no. 4, pp. 889–907.

Telegraph Women's Sport 2019, 'Introducing *Telegraph* Women's Sport: A new era of unprecedented coverage', 18 March, viewed 19 March 2019, <https://www.telegraph.co.uk/womens-sport/2019/03/18/introducing-telegraph-womens-sport-new-era-unprecedented-coverage/>.

Thompson, C 2006, *The Tour de France: A Cultural History,* University of California Press, Berkeley.

Tuchman, G 1972, 'Objectivity as strategic ritual: An examination of newsmen's notions of objectivity', *American Journal of Sociology,* vol. 77, no. 4, pp. 660–679.

Tunstall, J 1995, 'Specialist correspondents: Goals, careers, roles', in O Boyd-Barrett & C Newbold (eds), *Approaches to Media: A Reader,* Hodder Arnold, London, pp. 287–293.

Van Heekeren, M 2010, 'News in "new media": An historical comparison between the arrival of television and online news in Australia', *Media International Australia,* vol. 34, no. 1, pp. 20–30.

Vincent, J & Kian, E 2013, 'Sport, new media, and national identity', in ABM Hardin (ed), *Routledge Handbook of Sport and New Media,* Routledge, Abingdon and Oxfordshire, pp. 299–310.

Vos, T, Eichholz, M & Karaliova, T 2019, 'Audiences and journalistic capital', *Journalism Studies,* vol. 20, no. 7, pp. 1009–1027.

Walker, A 2006, 'Reporting play', *Journalism Studies,* vol. 7, no. 3, pp. 452–462.

The Walkley Foundation 1999, Malcolm Conn, https://www.walkleys.com/awards/walkley-winners-archive/.

Ward, M 2016, 'Seven West Media's acquisition of News Corp's *Sunday Times* and *Perth now* to be completed early next week', *Mumbrella,* 7 November, viewed 28 June 2018, <https://mumbrella.com.au/seven-west-medias-acquisition-news-corps-sunday-times-perthnow-completed-early-next-week-406565>.

Ward, T 2015, 'Aussies are sports mad, but Victorians are the clear winners', *The Conversation,* 13 August, viewed 12 November 2019, <http://theconversation.com/aussies-are-sports-mad-but-victorians-are-the-clear-winners-45761>.

Wasserman, H 2014, 'The ramifications of media globalization in the global south for the study of media industries', *Media Industries Journal*, vol. 1, no. 2, https://quod.lib.umich.edu/m/mij/15031809.0001.211?view=text;rgn=main.

Weaver, D & Wilhoit, G 1996, *The American Journalist in the 1990s: US News People at the End of an Era*, Lawrence Erlbaum Associates, Mahwah, NJ.

Weedon, G & Wilson, B 2017, 'Textbook journalism? Objectivity, education and the professionalization of sports reporting', *Journalism*, pp. 1–26. DOI:10.1177/1464884917716503.

Wei, W 2019, 'De-professionalism of sports journalism in post-truth era', paper presented to the *International Forum on Sports Communication*, Chengdu Sport University, Chengdu, China, 15–17 November.

White, D 1950, 'The "gatekeeper": A case study in the selection of news', *Journalism Quarterly*, vol. 27, no. 3, pp. 383–390.

Wingard, C 2020, 'I would love to see AFL players showing that kind of personality', *Hawthorn Football Club*, viewed 29 April 2020, <https://www.hawthornfc.com.au/news/587573>.

Wisden 2019, 'Cricket South Africa CEO apologises for "accreditation blunder"', viewed 5 February 2020, <https://www.wisden.com/stories/news-stories/cricket-south-africa-ceo-apologises-for-accreditation-blunder>.

Worlds of Journalism Study 2016, *Master Questionnaire, 2012–14*, viewed 12 June 2018, <https://worldsofjournalism.org/wojwordpress/wp-content/uploads/2019/07/WJS_core_questionnaire_2.5.1_consolidated.pdf>.

Young, M & Banks, A 2018, 'Foxtel CEO promises cricket fans he will "revolutionise TV cricket" like never before', *News.com.au*, 13 April, viewed 13 April 2018, <https://www.news.com.au/sport/breaking-news/foxtel-ceo-promises-cricket-fans-he-will-revolutionise-tv-cricket-like-never-before/news-story/6be8ed01a0c66a2a31cf584bf9b19e23>.

Zion, L, Spaaij, R & Nicholson, M 2011, 'Sport media and journalism: An introduction', *Media International Australia*, vol. 140, pp. 80–83.

Index

Milton Keynes UK
Ingram Content Group UK Ltd.
UKHW020849100524
442441UK00016B/125